"If you've ever wished for a clear and articulate overview that demystifies essential psychoanalytic ideas, this is it. Much more than an introduction, Ben Tyrer meticulously maps out the historical developments (and their misapplications) of psychoanalytic film theory to outline a more intersectional and accurate way of psychoanalytic film thinking. This excellent work reaffirms the critical importance of psychoanalysis for the study of the moving image, showing that a new way of 'psychoanalytic film thinking' is not only necessary but also essential if we are to properly understand film experience".

Professor Kelli Fuery, author of *Wilfred Bion, Thinking and Emotional Experience with Moving Images* (Routledge, 2018)

"With admirable clarity Tyrer takes readers on a comprehensive and fascinating journey through the key arguments of psychoanalytic film theory. Tyrer demonstrates that psychoanalytic approaches to films and cinema are needed today more than ever, and he reflects on aspects of spectatorship, race, sexuality, the cinematic gaze, and ideology, while charting the development of psychoanalytic film theory from the 1960s to the present. Impressive accounts are provided of key thinkers such as Christian Metz, Laura Mulvey, Slavoj Žižek, Todd McGowan, and others. The book should be essential reading for students as well as established film scholars"

Professor Richard Rushton, *Lancaster Institute for the Contemporary Arts, Lancaster University, UK*

Psychoanalytic Film Theory

In *Psychoanalytic Film Theory: A Contemporary Introduction*, Ben Tyrer presents an overview of psychoanalytic approaches to screen media, offering a reconsideration of psychoanalytic film theory while making the case for new forms of psychoanalytic film thinking.

Tyrer takes a series of key psychoanalytic concepts – including dream, identification, difference, object, and ideology – and charts their development in, and impact on, film theory. Considering foundational essays by Jean-Louis Baudry, Christian Metz, Laura Mulvey, and Jacqueline Rose, and contemporary conversations on cinema in the work of Joan Copjec, Slavoj Žižek, Alenka Zupančič, and Todd McGowan, the book considers the major insights and accomplishments of psychoanalytic film theory in contemporary context while offering a view of the intellectual life of psychoanalysis outside the clinic. Paying close attention to filmmakers such as Andrea Arnold, Joanna Hogg, Boots Riley, Celine Sciamma, and Wong Kar Wai, Tyrer demonstrates the continued importance of psychoanalysis when thinking about film and the pertinence of psychoanalytic film theory beyond its historical focus on classical Hollywood cinema.

Articulating complex ideas in an accessible way, this book is a vital starting point for students and scholars approaching psychoanalytic film theory for the first time, as well as scholars and analysts wishing to expand their knowledge and enhance their practice.

Ben Tyrer is a Lecturer in Film Theory at Middlesex University in London, UK. He is the author of books and articles on film, philosophy, and psychoanalysis, and the co-editor of *Femininity and Psychoanalysis: Cinema, Culture, Theory* (2019) and *Psychoanalysis and the Unrepresentable: From Culture to the Clinic* (2016).

Routledge Introductions to Contemporary Psychoanalysis

Series Editor: Aner Govrin
Executive Editor: Yael Peri Herzovich

Schizophrenia: A Contemporary Introduction
Gillian Steggles

Erotic Transferences: A Contemporary Introduction
Andrea Celenza

Otto Kernberg: A Contemporary Introduction
Frank Yeomans, Diana Diamond, Eve Caligor

Erich Fromm: A Contemporary Introduction
Sandra Buechler

Narcissism: A Contemporary Introduction
Richard Wood

The Death Drive: A Contemporary Introduction
Rossella Valdrè

Depression: A Contemporary Introduction
Marianne Leuzinger-Bohleber

Ronald Fairbairn: A Contemporary Introduction
David P. Celani

Depression: A Contemporary Introduction
Marianne Leuzinger-Bohleber

The Evidence for Psychodynamic Psychotherapy: A Contemporary Introduction
Kevin McCarthy, Carla Capone and Liat Leibovich

Psychoanalytic Group Psychotherapy: A Contemporary Introduction
Richard M. Billow

Existential Psychoanalysis: A Contemporary Introduction
M. Guy Thompson

Dreams and Dream Interpretation: A Contemporary Introduction
Christian Roesler

Interpersonal Psychoanalysis: A Contemporary Introduction
Anna Maria Loiacono

Psychodynamic and Psychoanalytic Supervision: A Contemporary Introduction
Christine Driver

Couple Relations: A Contemporary Introduction
Mary Morgan

The Oedipus Complex: A Contemporary Introduction
Poul Rohleder

Psychoanalytic Film Theory: A Contemporary Introduction
Ben Tyrer

Thomas Ogden: A Contemporary Introduction
Ofrit Shapira-Berman

For more information about this series, please visit: www.routledge.com/Routledge-Introductions-to-Contemporary-Psychoanalysis/book-series/ICP

Psychoanalytic Film Theory

A Contemporary Introduction

Ben Tyrer

LONDON AND NEW YORK

Designed cover image: © Michal Heiman, Asylum 1855–2020, The Sleeper (video, psychoanalytic sofa and Plate 34), exhibition view, Herzliya Museum of Contemporary Art, 2017

First published 2026
by Routledge
4 Park Square, Milton Park, Abingdon, Oxon OX14 4RN

and by Routledge
605 Third Avenue, New York, NY 10158

Routledge is an imprint of the Taylor & Francis Group, an informa business

© 2026 Ben Tyrer

The right of Ben Tyrer to be identified as author[/s] of this work has been asserted in accordance with sections 77 and 78 of the Copyright, Designs and Patents Act 1988.

All rights reserved. No part of this book may be reprinted or reproduced or utilised in any form or by any electronic, mechanical, or other means, now known or hereafter invented, including photocopying and recording, or in any information storage or retrieval system, without permission in writing from the publishers.

Trademark notice: Product or corporate names may be trademarks or registered trademarks, and are used only for identification and explanation without intent to infringe.

British Library Cataloguing-in-Publication Data
A catalogue record for this book is available from the British Library

Library of Congress Cataloging-in-Publication Data
Names: Tyrer, Ben author
Title: Psychoanalytic film theory : a contemporary introduction / Ben Tyrer.
Description: Abingdon, Oxon ; New York : Routledge, 2026. | Series: Routledge introductions to contemporary psychoanalysis | Includes bibliographical references and index. |
Identifiers: LCCN 2025031241 (print) | LCCN 2025031242 (ebook) | ISBN 9781032503233 paperback |
ISBN 9781032507644 hardback | ISBN 9781003399544 ebook
Subjects: LCSH: Psychoanalysis and motion pictures |
LCGFT: Film criticism
Classification: LCC PN1995.9.P783 T97 2026 (print) |
LCC PN1995.9.P783 (ebook) | DDC 791.4301/9–dc23/eng/20250801
LC record available at https://lccn.loc.gov/2025031241
LC ebook record available at https://lccn.loc.gov/2025031242

ISBN: 978-1-032-50764-4 (hbk)
ISBN: 978-1-032-50323-3 (pbk)
ISBN: 978-1-003-39954-4 (ebk)

DOI: 10.4324/9781003399544

Typeset in Times New Roman
by Taylor & Francis Books

For the dreamers who dream and then live inside the dream ...

Contents

List of Figures		xii
Series Editor's Preface		xiii
ANER GOVRIN		
	Psychoanalysis and Cinema: A Reintroduction	1
1	Dream	8
2	Identification	18
3	Difference	40
4	Object	64
5	Ideology	96
6	Conclusion: Psychoanalytic Film Thinking	122
	Recommended Reading	127
	Bibliography	128
	Index	135

Figures

0.1	*The Souvenir Part II* – Possibilities of meaning	2
1.1	*The Spirit of the Beehive* – Magic of the dream-cave	12
2.1	*Le Quattro Volte* – Goat identification	26
2.2	*Atlantics* – Hauntings of global capital	33
3.1	*Transformers* – Halting the narrative	47
3.2	*Portrait of a Lady on Fire* – Horizonal desire	53
3.3	*Casino Royale* – Spectacular masculinities	58
4.1	*The Pervert's Guide to Cinema* – Žižek in the picture	81
4.2	*In the Mood for Love* – Loving the obstacle	85
4.3	*Red Road* – Impossible encounter	94
5.1	*Sorry to Bother You* – Promise of capitalist enjoyment	113
6.1	*Barbie* – Looking the negative in the face	123

Series Editor's Preface

Aner Govrin

Routledge Introductions to Contemporary Psychoanalysis is one of the most prominent psychoanalytic publishing ventures of our day. The series' aim is to become an encyclopedia of psychoanalysis, with each entry given its own book.

This comprehensive series illuminates the intricate landscape of psychoanalytic theory and practice. In this collection of concise yet illuminating volumes, we delve into the influential figures, groundbreaking concepts, and transformative theories that shape the contemporary psychoanalytic landscape.

At the heart of each volume lies a commitment to clarity, accessibility, and depth. Our expert authors, renowned scholars and practitioners in their respective fields, guide readers through the complexities of psychoanalytic thought with precision and enthusiasm. Whether you are a seasoned psychoanalyst, a student eager to explore the field, or a curious reader seeking insight into the human psyche, our series offers a wealth of knowledge and insight.

Each volume serves as a gateway into a specific aspect of psychoanalytic theory and practice. From the pioneering works of Sigmund Freud to the innovative contributions of modern theorists such as Antonino Ferro and Michal Eigen, our series covers a diverse range of topics, including seminal figures, key concepts, and emerging trends. Whether you are interested in classical psychoanalysis, object relations theory, or the intersection of neuroscience and psychoanalysis, you will find a wealth of resources within our collection.

One of the hallmarks of our series is its interdisciplinary approach. While rooted in psychoanalytic theory, our volumes draw upon insights from psychology, philosophy, sociology, and other disciplines to offer a holistic understanding of the human mind and its complexities.

Each volume in the series is crafted with the reader in mind, balancing scholarly rigor with engaging prose. Whether you are embarking on your journey into psychoanalysis or seeking to deepen your understanding of specific topics, our series provides a clear and comprehensive roadmap.

Moreover, our series is committed to fostering dialogue and debate within the psychoanalytic community. Each volume invites readers to critically engage with the material, encouraging reflection, discussion, and further exploration.

We invite you to join us on this journey of discovery as we explore the ever-evolving landscape of psychoanalysis.

Aner Govrin

Psychoanalysis and Cinema
A Reintroduction

A group of students drink and dance in a small flat. Celebratory cake is cut. Soul II Soul's "Back to Life" fills the room. Suddenly, we are outside the flat looking in through a window. Except now we see that this is not a flat but a set, a construction on a soundstage, with performers inside. We move laterally, to the left, which reveals lighting stands, props, extras, camera equipment, and a film crew. A voice shouts, "Cut!", and the image reverts to black. Credits roll.

We begin at the end: with the final scene of Joanna Hogg's *The Souvenir Part II* (2021), where the director herself calls out to mark the conclusion. Hogg's artistic intervention here should be compared to that of the analyst as the one who effectively yells "*Cut!*" to end a psychoanalytic session at an unexpected yet important point. In both instances, interruption gives us cause to (re)consider what has gone before and allows for new meanings to emerge (this being the rationale for Lacan's "variable length session", wherein the analyst could call a halt at any time rather than simply enduring the officially prescribed 50-minute appointment). In introducing the *cut* here, cinema and psychoanalysis alike create an intervention in the flow of affects and signifiers, opening up possibilities for different kinds of storytelling about the self: the analysand asks, *What did I say (or not say) to bring the session to a halt today?*; the spectator of Hogg's film wonders, *What did I just witness? A recuperative fiction of remembering, repeating and working through, or a fantasy of trauma overcome?*.

This ambiguity is felt particularly in the brief tracking shot (Fig. 0.1), late in the film, of Julie running through the Norfolk countryside as Annie Lennox sings of "bliss" on the soundtrack. This might be read as a joyful return to reality after the high artifice of the film-within-a-film representing Julie's final year project, a cathartic expression of release and healing through art after her boyfriend's death; but, seen in retrospect, from the disorienting return to self-reflexive artifice at the film's end, the warm music and bucolic imagery here indicate a degree of *excess* that might suggest a fantasmatic dimension to the scene. The "cut" of the film unpicks the thread of what Lacan called *capitonnage*, the effect of an upholsterer's stich holding signifier and signified together ([1981] 1993), allowing them to *run* once more. This book constitutes a similar gesture: an intervention in conversations around psychoanalysis and cinema, a *cut* in present discourses of psychoanalytic film theory that might reshape or reconfigure the past while opening possibilities for future enquiry.

Cinema and Psychoanalysis

Psychoanalysis is fundamental to how we think about cinema. From the end of the 19th century, when the Lumière brothers and Sigmund Freud each unveiled their groundbreaking inventions –

Figure 0.1 The Souvenir Part II – Possibilities of meaning

cinématographe, Traumdeutung – through to the Surrealists, Alfred Hitchcock, Maya Deren, Christopher Nolan, David Lynch, Carol Morley, and Sarah Polley in the decades that followed, fantasy, dream, and screen have been inextricably linked.[1] With early precursors in the work of Raymond Bellour (collected in 2000) and the *Cahiers du cinéma* text on *Young Mr Lincoln* ([1970] 1972), psychoanalytic film theory emerged in the latter half of the 20th century as a major discourse in media scholarship and played a vital role in establishing Film Studies as an academic discipline.

Freud records his own encounter with the moving image – in the proto-cinematic technology of the "magic lantern" – while holidaying in Rome in 1907. In a letter home, he describes "suffer[ing] quietly the advertisements and monotonous photographs" while being "spellbound" by the "short cinematographic performances" (1975: 261–2). Cinema continues to be an object of fascination for the analytic community, as demonstrated by contemporary clinicians such as Anouchka Grose (2018) and Andrea Sabbadini (2014).[2] My aim with this book, therefore, is to speak directly to this mutual fascination and take it further by bringing the perspectives of contemporary psychoanalytic theory and contemporary cinema to bear on the complex intellectual history of these interactions. Such captivating analytical perspectives can be further enriched by the deep insights into past and present conversations between psychoanalysis and cinema that film theory provides, and this introduction will offer a resource for anyone with a psychoanalytic orientation who wants to consider the moving image in detail. This book will also offer a view of the intellectual life of psychoanalysis *outside* of the clinic, where the field of Film Studies has arguably been responsible for the broader dissemination of Freud's ideas. In the UK and USA, one is perhaps as likely to find psychoanalysis being taught in the Film and Media departments as the Psychology departments of the modern university.

Even so, psychoanalytic film theory has more recently fallen out of favour in the academy, replaced by cognitivism and neoformalism in mainstream scholarship and by a turn towards philosophy in more speculative approaches to the moving image: both defined in strict antagonism to psychoanalysis. In parallel, however, new strands of psychoanalytic thought have emerged, offering vital perspectives on the screen but also demonstrating how cinema itself can cast new light on psychoanalytic thinking in relation to the wider world. As such, this introduction is addressed also to media scholars of all types, from those encountering psychoanalytic film thinking for the first time to those who might now take for granted what this discourse had to offer as an historical curio and little else. In both instances, I hope to provide something novel, even something surprising in bringing cinema and psychoanalysis together *encore*, particularly as I endeavour to chart their intersections with wider critical thought.

Freud knew that psychoanalysis would – even *must* necessarily – meet with resistance, and nowhere has this been more true than in Film Studies. As we will see, hostility to psychoanalytic film theory was almost immediate, but what we will also see in the coming chapters is that psychoanalysis *is* the theory of resistance: of the circuitous paths that we will take to avoid the traumatic realisation of desire. In this way, we can appreciate psychoanalysis as an account of *why* we might be inclined to reject psychoanalysis itself.

We should also recognise how film theory today is characterised by a sort of Cartesian dualism in its organising metaphors: with work on film as mind/brain (Frampton, 2006; Pisters, 2012) on one side, and film as body (Sobchack, 1992; Shaviro, 1993; Marks, 2000) on the other. It is for this reason that the reintroduction of Freud is necessary. As Alenka Zupančič notes, the proper place of psychoanalysis is at the interface of the psychic and somatic: its object "is the zone where the two realms overlap". However, this is not simply a question of "two well-established entities ('body' and 'mind'), but an intersection which is generative of both sides that overlap in it" (2008: 7–8). A (re)turn to psychoanalytic film theory could offer unique perspectives on this intellectual landscape and offer new modes of analysis.[3]

Finally, it will be my claim that psychoanalysis is uniquely positioned to address the most pressing problems we face today. With an understanding of the unconscious (as what Freud called the "other scene", of desires and motivations of which we are usually unaware) and of enjoyment (as what Lacan called *jouissance*, or the satisfaction derived from pursuing these impulses, even while it might consciously be experienced as a kind of suffering), psychoanalysis gives us a convincing account of the seemingly irrational and even self-destructive tendencies we can observe around us, from the climate crisis to the rise of neo-fascism. In relation to this, we have accepted that films, like fairy tales and myths, can be *morally* instructive – giving us perspectives on the "good life" and how to lead it – but I will suggest that cinema can be *libidinally* instructive: giving us new perspectives on desire that fundamentally shift our relationship to the world.

Structure and Method

This book presents a new overview of psychoanalytic approaches to screen media, through a reconsideration of the existing field, exploration of recent developments, and insistence on the possibilities yet to come. In what follows, I take five key psychoanalytic themes – dream, identification, difference, object, ideology – and chart their development in and impact on film theory: from foundational essays by Jean-Louis Baudry, Christian Metz, Laura Mulvey, Jacqueline Rose, and Elizabeth Cowie, to contemporary conversations on cinema in the work of Joan Copjec, Slavoj Žižek, Alenka Zupančič, Todd McGowan, and others. This will require close attention to various films, both classic and contemporary, that offer vital perspectives on the questions at hand. The discussion will revisit some of those canonical figures referenced by the original psychoanalytic film theorists (e.g., Hitchcock) but will equally require consideration of new and wide-ranging cinematic trends in the work of filmmakers such as Michelangelo Frammartino, Andrea Arnold, Wong Kar Wai, Céline Sciamma, and Boots Riley. This expanded frame of reference will demonstrate the continued importance of psychoanalysis to thinking about film and the pertinence of psychoanalytic film theory beyond its historical focus on classical Hollywood cinema.

This will also be a contemporary introduction for how it situates psychoanalytic film theory in its wider context – primarily in its entanglements with Marxist, feminist, queer, postcolonial, and critical race theory – allowing me to demonstrate the on-going relevance of thinking psychoanalysis and cinema together. This will mean consideration of theorists such as bell hooks, Iris Brey, Sheldon George, Mark Fisher, and Lee Edelman (alongside those already mentioned) to examine the intersections and interactions of class, race, and sex in relation to cinema, as well as broadening the critical horizons of these traditional fields of enquiry.

In providing what I am tempted to call an "A-to-Z of psychoanalytic film theory" (from Apparatus to Žižek, but also beyond), it is necessary to acknowledge two final points. First, a distinction between *psychoanalytic film theory* as an historical phenomenon (e.g., the discourse around the *Screen* journal, conceptions of the "gaze") and contemporary *psychoanalytic film thinking* that has emerged in response to, or even against, the positions of that 1970s paradigm, as signalled by Copjec's vital intervention, "The Orthopsychic Subject: Film Theory and the Reception of Lacan".[4] I would align my own position with this latter paradigm – as pursuing an intellectual project that takes seriously Žižek's question, "what if one should finally give Lacan himself a chance [in Film Studies]?" (2001: 2) – but I will, nonetheless, also take seriously the concepts and contributions of Baudry, Metz, Mulvey et al. as vital to our understanding of both cinema and psychoanalysis.

Second, as a short study, the scope of this project is necessarily limited, and so I must make certain selections and omissions: my key decision is to focus mainly on the Freudian-Lacanian paradigm in film theory at the expense of other schools. We should certainly acknowledge vital, emergent discourses such as object relations film theory for their diverse contributions to the continued explorations of psyche and screen.[5] For its own part, however, this book will focus on work derived from Jacques Lacan's reinterpretation of Freud as that which has contributed most to the history of psychoanalytic film theory and continues to present the most significant psychoanalytic perspective on cinema.

In this way, I will make a claim for the continued relevance of psychoanalytic film theory even while the hegemonic discourses in the field would now deny it. For instance, Steven Shaviro's *The Cinematic Body* establishes itself explicitly in opposition to the psychoanalytic film theory of the 1970s to suggest that it is moribund; Vivian Sobchack's *The Address of the Eye* is presented as a movement beyond the "constraints" of this framework; and David

Bordwell and Noël Carroll's *Post-Theory* (1996) insists that psychoanalysis no longer has enough to offer film study (if, in their estimation, it ever did). These current trends in film analysis and film-philosophy – inspired by cognitive theory or Gilles Deleuze and Maurice Merleau-Ponty – seem to suggest that there is no place for psychoanalysis anymore. Arguing against such prevailing attitudes by drawing on a wealth of contemporary Freudian and Lacanian cine-writing, this book insists that, far from having passed, the time for psychoanalytic film theory is only just beginning.

Notes

1 Commentaries on psychoanalysis and cinema are fond of citing 1895 as the year when both were "born": the Lumière brothers screening their short "actualities" in the Café de Paris, and Freud and Breuer publishing *Studies on Hysteria*. There is, however, a degree of productive anachronism and apocrypha in this origin story: moving image technologies had been developed in diverse locations by several experimenters, with the Lumières likely being *the first to project moving images on a screen for a paying public*; and while Freud and Breuer did make a radical contribution to the psychology of sexuality and trauma, it is Freud's *Interpretation of Dreams* – famously completed in 1899 but dated 1900 in recognition of its paradigm-shifting intervention – that truly inaugurates psychoanalytic thinking.
2 Pioneering psychoanalyst Lou Andreas-Salomé suggested in 1913 that film should be of interest to the clinical field for what it might reveal about the psyche ([1913] 1964: 101).
3 See Tyrer (2022).
4 See also McGowan's *The Real Gaze* (2007a), a title punning on its theoretical significance (i.e., characterising the gaze as *objet a*, the little piece of the Real in the visual field) but also, by implication, presenting itself as the true or authentic (i.e., "real") theory of the gaze, against a false or inauthentic version offered by the *imaginary* gaze of "Screen theory".
5 See Sergeant (2021), Bainbridge (2019), Lebeau (2014), Kuhn (2013), Yates (2007) on Winnicott; and Fuery (2018), Ambrósio Garcia (2016) on Bion.

Chapter 1

Dream

A sense of connection between dream and cinema is as old as the medium itself: in his evocative report on an encounter with the Lumière projections in 1896, Russian writer Maxim Gorky described his entry into an oneiric "kingdom of shadows", "a world without sound, without colour", where "Strange imaginings invade your mind and your consciousness begins to wane and grow dim" ([1896] 1972: 3–6). The Surrealists, now working after Freud, saw art – and, for Germaine Dulac, Man Ray, Robert Desnos, Salvador Dali, and Luis Buñuel, *cinema* in particular – as a means of accessing the heightened reality of the unconscious that whispers to us in the dreamworld. Meanwhile, in the "dream factory" of Tinseltown, Alfred Hitchcock popularised a pulp Freudianism with his dreamlike narratives of repression and obsessive desires – from *Spellbound* (1945) to *Marnie* (1964) – while the titans of contemporary Hollywood continue to centre dream as a metaphor for filmmaking itself: Steven Spielberg famously naming his production company after Freudian *dreamwork*, Pixar's *Inside Out* spin-off *Dream Productions* (2024) dramatising this process, and Christopher Nolan's *Inception* (2010) casting dreamland architect Ariadne as a stand-in for the figure of the director as such.

Groundbreaking experimental filmmakers from Maya Deren to David Lynch and Apichatpong Weerasethakul have continued to explore the dream/screen affinity through works like *Meshes of the Afternoon* (1943), *Lost Highway* (1997), and *Cemetery of Splendour* (2015). While, most recently, Mark Cousins structures his film essay *The Story of Film: A New Generation* (2021) around a collection of "Dreamers", who go to sleep like they go to the movies, giving us a contemporary echo of that most crucial psychoanalytic consideration of the unique experience of cinema. This first chapter will therefore focus on two key moments in psychoanalytic film theory: the cinematic *dream-cave* evoked by Jean-Louis Baudry in the 1970s and what Slavoj Žižek calls the "screen of [our] dreams" – particularly where cinema represents itself – in his documentary, *The Pervert's Guide to Cinema* (2006), as ways of conceptualising the encounter between image and unconscious that film provides.

The Dream-Screen

In his landmark 1970 essay, "Ideological Effects of the Basic Cinematographic Apparatus", Baudry makes a passing observation that "The arrangement of different elements – projector, darkened hall, screen [... reproduces] in a striking way the *mise-en-scène* of Plato's cave" ([1970] 1974–1975: 45). He does not elaborate there, but clearly unable to escape the cave he returns to the topic more fully in "The Apparatus". Here, Baudry builds on what Gorky, the Surrealists, Deren and co. seemed instinctively to grasp – i.e., the striking similarities between cinema and dreaming – while also noting the concept of the "dream screen" introduced by American psychoanalyst Bertram Lewin as a cinematic metaphor for the "blank background" against which dreams put desire into motion ([1975] 1976: 116). Such affinities, Baudry suggests, are compelling but require further investigation.

He goes on to consider the "impression of reality" (104) in cinema and dream through Freudian psychoanalysis and Platonic philosophy. Book VII of *The Republic* describes a scene in which prisoners in a cave are chained with their back to the fire so all they can see are shadows on the wall. For Plato, this was an allegory for those ignorant of his theory of forms; but, with Baudry, we can find an uncanny rendering of the layout of the modern cinema and, more importantly, we can recognise the significance for film theory of the prisoners' error in mistaking an appearance (a *shadow on the wall*) for reality.

To explore this question, Baudry compares Plato with Freud as they each distribute knowledge across two different locations: the cave and the outside world for the former, and the conscious and unconscious for the latter. Baudry insists that they cannot be mapped directly, but he seems to suggest we can find a sort of inverse relation between them: if Plato insisted that we must leave the cave to discover the sun and the true nature of reality, then Freud suggests that the true reality of the human subject resides, as it were, *within the cave*. Freud's moment of enlightenment is to move into the epistemological *darkness* of the unconscious, along the *via regia* of the interpretation of dreams.

Baudry notes that dreaming eases the distinction between conscious and unconscious and allows mental images to take on the apparent status of sensory perceptions for dreamers. In dreams, we see without sight, hear without audition: *in dreams, the mind becomes our reality*. This is in part because we cannot dispel the reality of the dream. We test our perceptions through action: if we can interact with a perception – if I can touch this keyboard before me – then it is taken as external; if not, it must be an hallucination. Dreaming denies us this test, so a kind of hallucination is taken as our reality. In fact, it is "more-than-real" (118) because the dream submerges the dreamer totally in its image world.

The dream puts us into a state of regression. It takes us back to a stage where, as infants, we lacked understanding of the distinction between ourselves and the world: between perception through the senses and representation in the mind, or between reality and fantasy. This is where Baudry finds a parallel with cinema, which he characterises as a cave-like apparatus for the simulation of (psychic) reality. Baudry asserts that the impression of reality in cinema does not depend on the form or content of a particular film but on a mental interaction between cinema and the individual in the *event of spectatorship*. It is this conjunction *in its totality* – viewer, cinema space, projection technology – that Baudry calls the "apparatus". In considering this triad, he argues, theoretical approaches have so far not considered the role of the *unconscious*. Baudry attempts to address this question through a *psychoanalysis of spectatorship*.

The cinematic experience takes us into a state of artificial regression through its similarity to a dream-state, as we become passive and immobile before a moving image: like the prisoner, we tend to remain in our seats, eyes fixed on the screen. This regression is motivated by a desire to return to an earlier, infantile satisfaction. It is like dreaming because there is a similar loss of distinction between the person and the world, and because of the intensity with which the spectator attaches to the images. This turns the cinema-cave into a dream space, an effect reinforced by what Baudry calls a "partial elimination of the reality test" (120). The dreamer may wake up from the dream and the spectator may leave the cinema, but in neither case can they act *upon* the images as we can with empirical objects. The cinema is thus a simulation machine in which the unfolding of the film image *imposes* itself upon the spectator like a dream so that the spectator develops an overwhelming impression of reality that is similarly "more-than-real".

As with the allegory of the cave, this puts into question the relation between perception and representation (or image). In the cinema, we remain *conscious* but relate to our perception of the world as we would in the *unconscious*, so that perception of an image on screen is taken for perception of reality. And if the dream, for Freud, was a "normal hallucinatory psychosis", then the cinema, according to Baudry, is an "artificial psychosis" (121), a *simulation* of the dream-state. According to Freud, dreamwork turns our thoughts, memories, and desires into images. Sleep puts these dream images in the place of our senses as our reality. Cinema simulates this process to provide a real image that appears to us *like* an hallucination. The film seems like a dream, and it is this blurring of perception and hallucination that ultimately brings about the impression of reality that Baudry finds in cinema spectatorship. We invest in the perceptual images of the cinema like we do in dreams, and so these images similarly take over our reality.

We are child-like dreamers before the screen. We experience sounds and images – *an impression of reality* – more powerfully than our own true sense of reality. Cinema unlocks our desires like a dream and envelops us with its sensations: a cave-like experience nowhere better demonstrated than in Victor Erice's magical realist psychological drama, *The Spirit of the Beehive* (1973). A travelling projectionist comes to a rural Spanish village just after the Civil War, and young Ana and her sister Isabel see their first film: James Whales' *Frankenstein* (1931). As Rob Stone describes,

> Erice cuts back and forth between a frontal shot of the audience and a gradual zoom-in to the screen from their perspective. This zoom breaks down the distance between the audience and the film and thereby anticipates the central quandary of Ana: her inability to distinguish between reality and fantasy.
>
> (2014: 88)

What follows is a revelatory moment – the incredible power of cinema as *more-than-real* writ large across Ana's face – as she is first enraptured, then horrified by the monster's story: eyes widening and mouth agape as if what she is seeing is really happening (Fig. 1.2).

It is a moment of pure absorption in the film image: an experience so overwhelming that Ana subsequently interprets the world around her through this encounter with cinema as she imagines meeting the monster in the Spanish countryside. In fact, this scene further confuses our own distinctions between fantasy and reality,

Figure 1.1 The Spirit of the Beehive – Magic of the dream-cave

screen and world, when we realise that this was not "acting" but an authentic moment: Erice reports that this really was young Ana Torrent's first experience of seeing a film, and her total immersion in the spectacle was her genuine response to the moving image (Stone, 2014: 90). For Baudry, we all become Ana when we enter the dream-cave of cinema and are, as children, swept up by the magic of the apparatus.

Yet, Baudry notes an important, final distinction between dream and cinema. Whereas in dreams mental images appear to us like external reality, in the cinema, external reality appears to us like a dream. Dreams are taken as reality in the *absence* of perception, while cinema is taken for a dream-like reality *through* perception itself. Cinema, in the final analysis, is *not* a dream but provokes a similar effect: it creates a position for the viewer that simulates the experience of dreaming. Nonetheless, Baudry concludes with a final return to the cave, noting that the fact that Plato conjured a structure so like the cinema over 2,000 years ago suggests that the desire to invent cinema is an ancient one. The emergence of film attests to the presence of the unconscious because it is a representation *of* the unconscious: human endeavour from Plato to the Lumières involves the creation of analogues of the human psyche, of apparatus which mimics the functioning of the mind. In a properly Freudian manner, we could say that the unconscious might not be directly available to empirical observation, but its effects can be discerned from the very fact of the cinema itself.[1]

Cinema Dreams Itself

Baudry's vision of cinema is of course both historically and socially limited. On the one hand, he can be forgiven for not anticipating technological changes in television, streaming, and multiscreen viewing experiences that do not conform to the cave schema. On the other, Baudry's paradigm relies on an image of the silent, respectful darkness of bourgeois cinema unfamiliar to multiplex patrons and participants in more active and politically radical screenings such as the "Third Cinema" tradition alike.[2] Nonetheless, the persistence of the rarefied black-box space of the cinema in the cultural imaginary suggests its psychic resonance as identified in Baudry's thought.

Cinema is replete with such reflexive, magical-infantile moments of cinephilic absorption. Lynne Ramsay's *Ratcatcher* (1999), for example, uses the frame-within-a-frame device to evoke the dimensions of the cinema screen within the image itself as protagonist 12-year-old James escapes the drab streets of Glasgow for another world in the countryside. When he takes a bus out of town, the world passes before him, with each "frame" of the vehicle's panoramic window becoming like a cinema screen opening out onto realities he could never have imagined. When he discovers an abandoned housing estate, the effect is repeated as James climbs through an unfinished window, passing from bare plaster walls into an idyllic wheat field. The sudden introduction of music in these moments reminds us of their cinematic "artificiality" but draws us in, nonetheless. We are like Dorothy moving from the world of sepia to Technicolor Oz, but also like Buster Keaton's *Sherlock Jr.* (1924), whose hero steps from the auditorium *into* the world of the screen. It is a moment repeated in *Paddington* (2014), as the adventurous bear shuffles into a film projection to find the fantastical memory of his childhood Peru stored within the celluloid, reminding us again of the Baudrian dreamwork that follows our entrance into the cinema.

The Screen of Our Dreams

Žižek is particularly interested in these moments of meta-cinematic reflection, where films consider their own capacity to transform reality. Like Baudry, Žižek focuses on the question of screen and dream, but where Baudry explicitly did *not* engage with the specifics of any given work, Žižek offers close analysis of films that speak to the nature of cinematic aesthetics. In his essay, "The Thing from Inner Space", Žižek notes Lacan's claim in Seminar VII that "art as such is always organized around the central Void of the impossible-real Thing" and identifies a motif whereby this Thing "appears in the diegetic space of the cinematic narrative" (1999). Žižek offers several instances from science fiction films, such as the star destroyer piercing the void of space in the opening of *Star Wars* (1977) – a cinematic evocation of the metaphysical question, *Why is there something rather than nothing?* – and both the giant machine beneath the surface in *Forbidden Planet* (1956) and the planet itself in Tarkovsky's *Solaris* (1972). These latter examples are particularly important for Žižek as the manifestation of the "Thing as an Id-Machine, a mechanism that directly materializes our unacknowledged fantasies" (1999).

He concludes that Tarkovsky's emphasis on earthly textures across his work – particularly *Solaris* and *Stalker* (1979) – constitutes the Thing as "[giving] body to the direct coincidence of Matter and Spirit". He continues,

> In a homologous way, Tarkovsky displaces the common notion of dreaming, of entering a dream: in Tarkovsky's universe, the subject enters the domain of dreams not when he loses contact with the sensual material reality around him, but, on the contrary, when he abandons the hold of his intellect and engages in an intense relationship with material reality. The typical stance of the Tarkovskian hero on the threshold of a dream is to be on the lookout for something, with the attention of his senses fully focused; then, all of a sudden, as if through a magic transubstantiation, this most intense contact with material reality changes it into a dreamscape.
>
> (1999)

Žižek revisits this idea of entering the film-dream through his own cinematic encounter in *The Pervert's Guide to Cinema*. After an introduction which declares cinema to be "the ultimate pervert art" – because it does not give us *what* we desire but tells us instead *how* to desire – the film turns our attention to Clarence Brown's Hollywood melodrama, *Possessed* (1931): a young woman watches a train pass slowly before her, and through the windows she sees different strata of social life – cooks, waiters, maids, and high class couples – with each scene framed like images on a celluloid strip moving through the projector. Žižek notes that "All of a sudden she finds herself in a situation where reality itself reproduces the magic cinematic experience": she becomes another cinematic spectator, like Ana, like James, like ourselves. A man leans out from the train and offers her a drink, telling her that it is far better to get in and look out than to look in. As Žižek explains,

> We get a very real, ordinary scene onto which the heroine's inner space, as it were, her fantasy space is projected, so that, although all reality is simply there, the train, the girl, part of reality in her perception and in our viewer's perception is, as it were, elevated to the magic level, becomes the screen of her dreams. This is cinematic art at its purest.

There is an echo of Baudry here, in Žižek's observation that the power of cinema is to make reality seem like a dream – a perception for a fantasy – which runs counter to the common-sense idea that moving images make an illusion seem real. Like the "Thing from inner space", the train – as both real object within the diegesis and analogue for cinema itself – seems to manifest, to put into motion, her desire.

Žižek later draws these strands together in *Disparities*, where he traces the effect back to Charles Dickens. Rather than the departure from reality in the Freudian dream of the burning son – where the father enters the dream, only to encounter the traumatic Real of his child's reproach – "in Dickens, there is no escape from ordinary reality, a detail of reality itself gets spectralized, is experienced as a moment from a nightmarish dream" (2016a: 187). Žižek then turns to an unexpected shot from *Titanic* (1997) showing an elderly couple in bed as they are engulfed by water, which provides "an authentic cinematic touch, that of making reality appear as a dream scene" (187). This Žižek relates back to *Possessed* but also to Krzysztof Kieslowski, who – like Dickens – could make mundane material objects and events hyperreal by "[stirring] up in my 'inner life' – not some 'deeper meaning' but something traumatic, nonsymbolizable, ex-timate (external in the very heart of my being)" (188). For Žižek, this dreamwork of cinema reveals not the postmodern fiction of reality but the reality of fiction itself.

Emphasising dreams at the outset of this project highlights the central importance of *form* to both psychoanalysis and cinema.

Freudian technique is a formal practice that, rather than dwelling on content, attends to the *shape* of its problems (dreams, symptoms) as they are determined/distorted by unconscious desire. And while Baudry was more interested in the experiences and technologies of cinema projection than the specifics of a film's audio-visual style, many of the central concepts of psychoanalytic film theory to be elaborated in what follows *are* centred on form: the "male gaze" and "suture", for instance, are theories of classical Hollywood aesthetics as much as they are theories of spectatorship and metapsychology; and the most vital, contemporary psychoanalytic film thinking puts the question of form at its centre. As we will see, what Žižek identifies as cinema's own mode of thought is precisely in the tension between content and form. For now, however, we will continue in the field of cinematic spectatorship by turning to the problem of *identification*.

Notes

1 McGowan notes that film production and viewing involves multiple subjects, so it is a "collective dream [which] reveals more precisely the psyche as such than any individual's dream does" (2015: 2).
2 Third Cinema: a political film movement originating in Latin America that encourages an active, critical attitude towards the screen, turning film screenings into social events outside traditional cinemas.

Chapter 2

Identification

A meme titled "The 'you missed the point by idolizing them' Starter Pack" was posted on social media in 2019. Under this text, the meme included images of pop culture figures such as Patrick Bateman, Travis Bickle, Jordan Belfort, Walter White, Tyler Durden, Don Draper, Joaquin Phoenix's Joker, and *Watchmen*'s Rorschach.[1] The meme's message was characteristically clear – that these anti-heroes and villainous protagonists should *not* be considered role models for our everyday life – and its appearance seemed to be in response to the outgrowth of a certain section of Internet fandom expressing admiration for these figures, which overlapped at least to some extent with the so-called "manosphere" of online misogyny seeking to draw in disenfranchised young men.

While such hateful male supremacism should be rejected outright, there have also been repeated moral panics around the corrupting influence of popular media: from the 1980s UK "video nasties" hysteria to the 2010s backlash against *Twilight*, reaching all the way back to the infamously libertine early days of Hollywood – most recently fictionalised in Damien Chazelle's *Babylon* (2022) – which prompted the introduction of the moralising Hays Code of censorship that shaped mainstream US cinema for almost half of the 20th century. At the centre of each of these episodes lies a concern with the relationship between cinema and spectator – and specifically the transformative impact that the cinematic encounter might have on us – that is shared by psychoanalytic film theory from those pioneering writers of the 1970s to the thinkers of today.

DOI: 10.4324/9781003399544-3

This chapter will take up another of the first key debates in the field: the relationship between cinema and spectator conceived in terms of the psychoanalytic notion of *identification* – particularly as defined by Sigmund Freud as the assimilation of one ego to another, and by Jacques Lacan as the transformation when a subject assumes an image – returning once again to Baudry's theory of apparatus but also moving beyond that paradigm to consider more recent reflections on historically specific and politically contentious film encounters. With this, we move from the metaphor of the screen as *dream*, to conceptualisation of the screen as *mirror*.[2]

The Screen-Mirror

The preceding chapter took as its point of departure Jean-Louis Baudry's comparison of the cinema experience with Plato's Cave and Freudian dreamwork to explore spectatorship and the unconscious. Yet something crucial was omitted from Baudry's observation, which reads as follows: "The arrangement of the different elements – projector, darkened hall, screen – in addition from [sic] reproducing in a striking way the mise-en-scene of Plato's cave […] *reconstructs the situation necessary to the release of the 'mirror stage' discovered by Lacan*" ([1970] 1974–1975: 45). This is a reference to Lacan's essay, "The Mirror Stage as Formative of the Function of the I as Revealed in Psychoanalytic Experience" ([1966] 2006: 75–81), which proposed a key moment of development, the "mirror stage", where the child meets an image outside itself: in a real mirror or another person. Lacan suggested that when infants encounter the apparent *completeness* of the mirror-image, it seems preferable (an "ideal-ego") to the *fragmented* experiences of their own, not-yet-coordinated body. The child thus takes on what Lacan calls this "specular image" in the mirror as their identity, giving them a feeling of mastery over their body. This *identification with the image* is transformative. It provides a new sense of self: the ego. Crucially, however, this "recognition" of the self in the mirror image is a *misrecognition*: it is not me but an image. My sense of identity is thus *alienated*: experienced through something outside myself, an other, and is therefore fundamentally *illusory*.

For Baudry, something similar happens in spectatorship. He begins "Ideological Effects of the Basic Cinematographic Apparatus" with an examination of the principles of monocular perspective – the transformation of 3D space into a 2D image through a single lens – upon which the apparatus is based. Baudry suggests that the cinematic image is constructed and presented to the spectator so that they experience themselves in/as an *ideal vantage point*. The film is addressed to me: I am the fixed end point of all meaning. What we call the "spectator" is in fact a *location to be occupied*, positioned as the physical and symbolic *centre* of the cinema experience. The world is offered up to me, with the camera providing a vision beyond the limits of the human body: I experience spectatorship as a free-floating eye, or what Baudry calls a "transcendental subject" ([1970] 1974–1975: 43), and I encounter scenes that appear to be constituted not just by this eye but for it – *for me*.

We will return to the obvious ideological implications of this situation in Chapter 5, but for now we should note that this process, Baudry insists, relies on *identification*. The apparatus provides an environment recreating the situation of the mirror stage – physical immobility and "predominance of the visual function" – so strikingly similar for Baudry that it seems "more than simple analogy" (45). He notes that cinema does not *reproduce* this "origin of the self" in the mirror-stage exactly but *verifies* it through repetition: the self finds an illusory place in the cinema through a restaging of the mirror encounter. Cinematic spectatorship entails the reproduction of internal reality rather than the external world, which facilitates our identification with its vision.

Baudry in fact suggests that there is a "double identification" here but frames it in a convoluted way. The "first" level of identification is with characters on screen: the common-sense idea that we relate to people and stories we see in films. Yet Baudry describes the "second level" as identification which "permits the appearance of the first and places it 'in action' – this is the transcendental subject". This second level must therefore be logically *prior* to the first level – *it makes it possible* – and so would seem to "come first" in our engagement with the screen. Perhaps Baudry designates it as secondary because it resides largely at the edges of conscious perception and so seems less apparent than our identifications with those on screen. In any case, Baudry insists that "the spectator identifies less with what is represented, the spectacle itself, than with what stages the spectacle": i.e., the apparatus (45). It is the act of seeing as such, rather than any particular content of what is seen, that is paramount in our encounter with what Baudry calls the "screen-mirror" (44).

This is, nonetheless, perfectly illustrated by the meta-cinematic spectacle of Hitchcock's *Rear Window* (1954), which gives us both the immobile spectator and the apparent power of an ideal viewing position. Confined to a chair due to his broken leg, photographer L. B. "Jeff" Jeffries is the quintessential spectator: kept at a distance from the scene of his apartment block, he becomes an all-seeing eye through the telescope-like long lens of his Exakta camera. This apparatus carries his vision beyond the limits of his own body and gives him seeming access to, and thus knowledge of, the world before him. The film shatters this illusion in that famous, thrilling moment when the suspect Thorwald catches sight of Jeff and *looks back*: not just at him but seemingly at the spectator directly – in a moment of profound identification with both the form and the content of the cinematic experience – as we are pinned to our seats by Thorwald's accusing stare. Baudry argues that such moments – which render the structures of spectatorship visible, reminding us of our identification with the apparatus – give us scope to resist ideological positioning, aligning this possibility with self-reflexive cinematic practices (e.g., showing the camera on screen, see Chapter 5); while ultimately *Rear Window* reaffirms the omniscience of this transcendental, surveilling look by showing Thorwald to be a murderer, just as Jeff supposed. Yet, as we will see in Chapter 4, a film like Andrea Arnold's *Red Road* (2006) further confounds this dynamic by rendering the visual field complex and unknowable even while positioning its protagonist Jackie in that Baudrian all-seeing position as a CCTV operator.

A Strange Mirror

Following on from Baudry is Christian Metz: a trailblazing cine-semiotician who subsequently turned his attention to Freud and Lacan. His work *The Imaginary Signifier* – a 1975 essay (English translation in *Screen*) developed into a book in 1977 (English, 1982) – poses a key question: "What contribution can Freudian psychoanalysis make to the study of the cinematic signifier?" (1982: 17). His answer was a wide-ranging theory of spectatorship and cinema that, like Baudry, considered film as dream, as well as voyeurism, fetishism, metaphor, and metonymy. Cinema is an "imaginary signifier" for Metz because, like a mirror's reflection, it presents an image that is compellingly present but absent at the same time – it is *just* an image, but it is still a real perception of an "artificial" object – and, like the Lacanian mirror in particular, it provides a site for identifications.

In fact, Metz first emphasises how cinema *differs* from the looking glass, in that the screen never reflects the image of the spectator's own body. It is specifically absent from the scene and thus not available as a point of identification. The apparatus is:

> A strange mirror, then, very like that of childhood, and very different. Very like, as Jean-Louis Baudry has emphasised [...], because during the showing we are, like the child, in a sub-motor and hyper-perceptive state; because, like the child again, we are prey to the imaginary, the double, and are so paradoxically through a real perception. Very different, because this mirror returns us everything but ourselves, because we are wholly outside it, whereas the child is both in it and in front of it.
>
> (49)

The *strangeness* of this mirror is reflected in the (possibly apocryphal) anecdote – relayed by Adam Curtis' short film *Paranoia and Moral Panics* (2010) – suggesting that disgraced former US President Richard Nixon "told his psychiatrist that when he looked in the mirror in the morning, there was no one there". For Curtis, this is evidence supporting his characterisation of Nixon as a "paranoid weirdo"; while his wider argument is that an atmosphere of fear and suspicion promoted by tabloid journalism has meant that "millions of us have become exactly like Richard Nixon". This again speaks to the question of the impact of media upon us, but it also echoes Winnicott's case study – highlighted by

Vicky Lebeau's essay on Winnicott's response to the Lacanian mirror stage – wherein a patient exclaimed, "Wouldn't it be awful […] if a child looked into the mirror and saw nothing!" (quoted in Lebeau, 2014: 175). A mirror that does not return our reflection should be a terrible thing: an indicator of psychosis or childhood trauma. On entering the cinema, the spectator should also *become Richard Nixon* before the strange mirror: and yet, for Metz, this is not what happens.[3]

He suggests that spectatorship depends upon us having *passed through* the mirror stage already: we are able to make sense of the cinematic spectacle because we have already formed an identity as an ego separate from the world, and do not therefore require the support of our own reflection in the mirror to relate to what we see there (although, the cinema *does* provide surrogates for our own image, as we will see). This leads Metz to his next question: if not our own image, then with what do we identify? His answer is the mechanism of the cinema itself: spectatorship begins with "identification with the camera" (1982: 49).

With what he calls "primary cinematic identification", Metz reworks many of Baudry's ideas on the metapsychology of cinematic experience but does so in a more systematic way. Metz similarly suggests that the apparatus positions the spectator as the ideal addressee of the image, inscribing them in "an all powerful position which is that of God" (49). Cinema allows the spectator to experience themselves as *ubiquitous*. The effect of the apparatus is to make the spectator feel as though the cinematic spectacle exists solely for their benefit as "a great eye and ear without which the perceived would have no one to perceive it [… :] it is I who make the film" (48).

Just as Baudry had done, Metz identifies this "all-perceiving" spectator as a "transcendental subject" and makes explicit that they are the "condition of possibility" of the cinema (48, 49). Metz suggests that this leads the spectator to identify "*with himself*, with himself as a pure act of perception": identifying effectively with their own look as it coincides with that of the camera, "which has looked before him at what he is now looking at" (49). Metz acknowledges that this is also really identification with the *projector* as representative of the camera within the auditorium. This explains why we are not simply astonished when the camera moves in a pan, track or zoom, while we ourselves have not moved. Via the projector, the spectator takes on the camera's vision as their own and is constituted once again as an all-perceiving subject beyond their own, empirical subjectivity. Again, not unlike Baudry, Metz suggests that it is not just a coincidence that the apparatus mirrors the structures of perception because cinema itself has been shaped by the conditions of the mirror stage: primary cinematic identification requires us to have passed through the mirror stage but so too, for Metz, does the invention of the moving image itself.

This mirror-screen produces the spectatorial ego as a "transcendental yet radically deluded subject" (52). This effect gives us insight into what Metz calls "idealism in cinematic theory": identified with the phenomenological approach of the *Cahiers du Cinéma* founding editor, André Bazin, who saw cinema not as a mirror but as a *window* revealing the world to us. Metz characterises this understanding of spectatorship as a description of "the 'feeling' of the *deluded ego* of the spectator" (52). Phenomenology gives an account of the *user experience* of the apparatus but tells us nothing of how this experience is produced. As a result, Metz concludes, "cinema *and* phenomenology in their common illusion of *perceptual mastery*" require further interrogation through psychoanalysis (53). This is the closest Metz comes to acknowledging that such primary cinematic identification should, according to Lacan, be a *misrecognition*. It is identification with an illusory image of coherence, rather than a true position of ubiquity. Metz, however, leaves this tantalising possibility undeveloped, even while these ideas will be among the key terms in the debate that is to follow. In *The Imaginary Signifier*, Metz moves instead to the question of secondary cinematic identifications.

He notes that, "Obviously the spectator has the opportunity to identify with the *character* of the fiction" (48). As we have seen, Metz's preoccupation with "the place of the spectator's ego" within the apparatus leads to his focus on primary cinematic identification, but our relation to *other people* on screen might seem to offer a more direct mirror relation in terms of likeness, idealisation, and misrecognition. Perhaps this apparent obviousness limits Metz's critical interest in the topic, as he spends little time considering this aspect of our relation to the screen; yet it is arguably this question that most occupies contemporary concerns with screen spectatorship more generally. Metz does not spell it out, but the psychological mechanism implied here relies both on that transformative mirror relation suggested by Lacan and, crucially, the fundamental interpersonal relationship, which, Freud observed, entails "the assimilation of one ego to another one, as a result of which the first ego behaves like the second in certain aspects, imitates it and in a sense takes it up into itself" (SE 22: 63). Secondary cinematic identification recognises the possibility (if not the necessity) of such "assimilation" of the spectator to the figures on the screen and the adoption of certain of their characteristics (usually temporarily) as our own: a phenomenon borne out by the surge in sales of red leather jackets after the release of *Fight Club* (1999) and sex toys following *Fifty Shades of Grey* (2015).

What is interesting about Metz's approach is that he emphasises the role of *film language* in establishing such identification and raises the question of identification *beyond the human* in cinema. Forming bonds with characters, of course, is not unique to cinema, but Metz notes that a key way in which it differs from theatre is in film's capacity to engage with the "inhuman", or as he puts it: "cinematic 'cosmorphism' [...] – sequences in which only inanimate objects, landscapes, etc. appear" (47). Metz might have in mind here the work of avant-garde filmmaker and theorist Jean Epstein, who developed a concept of "*photogénie*" as the almost magical capacity of cinematography to bring things to life: not necessarily in terms of trick photography or stop-motion animation, but through the generative power of the camera's vision itself, as demonstrated in the attention to objects and faces in *Coeur fidèle* (1923) and *La chute de la maison Usher* (1928).

This also suggests Michelangelo Frammartino's *Le Quattro Volte* (2010): an example of "slow" or "contemplative" cinema, its minimal narrative is inspired by Pythagoras' doctrine of the transmigration of souls (*metempsychosis*). The film follows first an elderly goatherd, then a newborn kid, a fir tree, and a mound of charcoal as they each flourish and expire in the Calabrian countryside. For his part, Metz seems to imply that the spectator identifies *despite* the absence of the human form in such instances, relying on the primary identification with the camera to account for our engagement. Yet *Le Quattro Volte* demonstrates how *secondary* identifications can establish, persist, or shift focus over the course of a spectatorial experience offering little conventional narrative or even human likeness.

The film opens a space to become invested in the quotidian struggles of the ailing farmer, to ponder the sustaining powers of the folk remedy that he collects from the church, and to feel a pang of sorrow when he perishes in the night. Equally, it may well trade on a degree of anthropomorphism in how it encourages concern for the young goat lost in the woods, but in its sustained perspective on the animal, the film offers a potential point of connection: permitting the spectator to psychically occupy its place, even as the kid lies down to die beneath a fir tree (Fig. 2.1). From this point on, the film progressively distances us from the anthropic perspective, as we see the tree felled and resurrected for a village festival, and then we watch a mound of its smouldering logs turning into charcoal. The film de-emphasises dialogue and physiognomy, putting human language and bodies alongside other sounds and things, allowing us – in some sense – to put ourselves in the place of a branch swaying in the wind or carbonising in the fire. Cinematic identification here – the taking on of aspects of the other through the screen – becomes a vehicle for reflection on transformation, interconnectedness, and broader ecological concerns.

Figure 2.1 Le Quattro Volte – Goat identification

More conventionally, such identification is promoted in narrative cinema by the use of specific filmic grammars, or what Metz – harking back to his cine-semiotic studies – calls "sub-codes" that are "responsible for suggesting to the spectator the vector along which his permanent identification with his own look [i.e., primary cinematic identification] should be extended temporarily inside the film" (54). Metz notes that cinematic structures of looking play a major role in connecting spectator to spectacle. The subjective point-of-view shot (i.e., a shot representing a character's vision, their optical perspective directly) suggests profound connection between the primary and secondary aspects of Metz's theory of cinematic identification. Such an image might be indicated first by a shot of the character looking at something offscreen and then a cut to an image of what they are looking at, this second shot being understood as their "point-of-view"; or it might take the form of an approximation of embodied vision, the camera literally representing human sight, this "subjective shot" indicated by camera movements analogous to the movements of the body, and it could be marked in how actors and things interact with the camera directly, as if relating to another person. The former technique is a common feature of conventional film grammars ("point-of-view cutting"), while the latter has an illustrious history from Abel Gance's silent *Napoleon* (1927) and Robert Montgomery's noir mystery *Lady in the Lake* (1947) to RaMell Ross' *Nickel Boys* (2024) or Gaspar Noé's psychedelic *Enter the Void* (2009), which – like Montgomery's film before it – is shot entirely from the optical perspective of the protagonist, Oscar, even to the extent of including brief flashes of black screen to mimic *blinking*.

What is significant about the point-of-view shot is how it renders both levels of cinematic identification simultaneously: we take the vision of the camera to be, in a sense, our own vision – *primary cinematic identification* – while we also align ourselves with a subject *within the film*, through their vision: a *secondary cinematic identification*. The sort of free-floating point-of-view that we get later in *Enter the Void* – it is, in effect, another film about the transmigration of souls – is both *subjective* (the character's field of vision) and, in a sense, *objective* (pure camera vision) in that it presents an impossible perspective from beyond the grave. It is, then, particularly suggestive of the all-perceiving "transcendental" subject of the apparatus that both Metz and Baudry theorised.

And yet, as Vivian Sobchack notes in her discussion of *Lady in the Lake*, a POV effect is not totalising (1992: 230–48): the awkward movements of the large camera in Montgomery's film and, I would add, the "blinking" frames of Noé are techniques that seemingly *should* serve to further entrench the identificatory bond with the camera/character but in fact render it too palpable, putting the effect of spectatorship at risk. Such *excesses* of film aesthetics both reveal and point to the limits of the insight of classical psychoanalytic film theory here. As Sobchack suggests – in a remarkably Lacanian way – the technique introduces, or perhaps lays bare, a *gap* in the cinematic encounter where we encounter the subject.

Reflections

"Apparatus theory" (Baudry and Metz) was hugely influential on Film Studies in this early period but was also hugely controversial. As we will see in the next chapter, some immediate responses to Baudry and Metz from within psychoanalytic film theory highlight the elision of difference (and *sexual difference* in particular) in their conceptualisation of spectatorship. While later, the turn away from psychoanalysis and towards philosophy in Film Studies took aim at Apparatus theory for its apparent inattention to questions of embodiment in screen encounters. Steven Shaviro's uncompromising stance was that the "stultifying orthodoxy" of psychoanalytic film theory should be rejected in favour of the paradigm of Deleuze and Guattari, Foucault, and Bataille to grasp the corporeal qualities of both spectator and image (1993: ix). Similarly, Vivian Sobchack rejected the seemingly disembodied spectator of Apparatus theory in favour of a theory of the "lived-body experience of vision in its entirety" (1992: 267) informed by Maurice Merleau-Ponty. And yet, as Sarah Cooper astutely observes, the account that Sobchack later gives of spectatorship as "embodied knowledge" – i.e., that her fingers *knew* that they were seeing fingers on the screen in the blurry, indistinct opening shot of Jane Campion's *The Piano* (1993), even before she consciously registered the outline of Ada's hand (Sobchack, 2004: 63) – could be understood as a form of *corporeal identification* with the image, returning us to the dynamics of body and vision in the primal Lacanian mirror, and back further still to the questions of embodiment and conversion that first animated Freud's enquiries into the unconscious (Cooper, 2008: 109).[4]

Identification is constantly undergoing transformation. As Sharon Willis observes, it is a process rather than a fixation: "it is likely to be mobile and intermittent, rather than consistent" and "need not be based on consciously perceived or desired resemblances; indeed, [identification] may come as a surprise, a disruptive moment whose effects are partial, provisional and unpredictable" (1993: 121). Where I want to focus in the remainder of this chapter is on two key areas of such disruptive cinematic identification: in the expansion of the psychoanalytic paradigm in relation to race and colonisation through Frantz Fanon and Diana Fuss; and in the rejection of psychoanalysis as such in mainstream Film Studies, in favour of "cognitive" approaches to spectatorship, focusing on spectator "sympathy" and frameworks of morality.

Identification/Colonisation

A footnote to Frantz Fanon's psychopathology of colonisation, *Black Skin, White Masks*, pictures the following cinematic encounter:

> Attend showings of a Tarzan film in the Antilles and in Europe. In the Antilles, the young Negro identifies himself de facto with Tarzan against the Negroes. This is much more difficult for him in a European theater, for the rest of the audience, which is white, automatically identifies him with the savages on the screen.
>
> ([1952] 2008: 118)

Fanon describes here a complex psychodynamics of spectatorship in the context of colonialism. He suggests that when watching a classical Hollywood film in a colonised country the black spectator *identifies with the white hero*; while, transposing this scene back into the heart of empire, the white European spectators *identify him* – the colonial subject – with the black "savages" who threaten the protagonist.

These cinematic scenes effectively present Fanon's thesis in microcosm: under colonialism – e.g., France's occupation of Algeria (1830–1962) – the traditions of the colonised are systematically devalued, and they are compelled to imitate the coloniser's culture instead, hence the donning of "white masks". This valorisation of whiteness is also a denigration of blackness: "A normal Negro child, having grown up within a normal family, will become abnormal on the slightest contact with the white world" (111). White society trains its subjects through cultural representation to associate blackness with wrongness; and in the colonial situation, this attitude is internalised by the colonised people, causing deep psychological harm and setting the scene for cinematic encounters such as Fanon's *Tarzan*. Moreover, while the colonised must wear the white mask, they are continually held at a distance from colonial society: told they are *"almost the same but not white"*, as Homi Bhabha observes (1984: 130), just as the European audience reminds Fanon's "young Negro" at the cinema.

Fanon continues this analysis in his landmark final text, *The Wretched of the Earth*. He describes the French occupiers' attempts to brainwash Algerian intellectuals through psychological torture: "to attack from the inside those elements that constitute the national consciousness" ([1961] 2011: 213–4), transforming them into collaborators with the colonial regime by making them repeatedly rehearse the arguments *for* colonisation and *against* Algerian independence. Diana Fuss describes this as enforced imitation aiming to realign the Algerians' identifications: to make the colonised think and act like the coloniser so they come to identify with the colonial project (1995: 153). Fanon of course charts the debilitating psychological effects of such colonial oppression, but if the aim of such torture were truly to *convert* the Algerian revolutionary, then the regime singularly failed in its objective: when the men were released, they simply returned to the struggle for independence. As Fuss explains, this violent attempt to produce an "identification with the aggressor" fails because "imitation alone is not sufficient" (153).

Keeping Fanon's example of *Tarzan* in mind, however, we can see how cinema might "succeed" where torture fails in producing identification. When the aggressor (represented by Tarzan) is held up as an *ideal* – in the imaginary sense of the other as specular image – rather than a cruelly superegoic figure, the colonised subject assimilates himself much more readily to the occupier's position. By mobilising the vectors of identification, *Tarzan* achieves in a matter of hours at the cinema what colonisers seemingly failed to do in weeks at the torture chamber. Manthia Diawara (1988) identifies such a logic at the foundations of modern Hollywood – D.W. Griffith's infamously racist epic, *The Birth of a Nation* (1915) – which situates the spectator to identify with whiteness *against* the "black threat": embodied by Gus (white Walter Long, performing in blackface), who is presented as a sexual predator driving virginal, white Flora to her death in a scene that inspired a resurgence in KKK violence following the film's release. Such racialised cinematic identifications continue to characterise contemporary media – particularly after 9/11 – in the Islamophobic fantasy of what Jack Shaheen calls the "reel bad Arab" ([2001] 2009) and in the neo-colonial heroics against the non-white other of *Iron Man* (2008) or *American Sniper* (2014).

The question of resistance to colonial oppression was central to Fanon's project. In "Algeria Unveiled", he discusses the French occupiers' efforts to prevent women wearing the veil as an attempt to "Europeanise" Algerians through erasure of culture. For Fanon, every veil lifted was a "negative expression of the fact that Algeria was beginning to deny herself" ([1959] 2007: 42) – i.e., an identification with the coloniser – and so the veil itself became a symbol of anti-colonial resistance. Yet the Algerian National Liberation Front (known by its French acronym, FLN) also reversed this dynamic for radical ends: using the symbol of colonial domination (unveiling) as a revolutionary weapon. As Fanon describes, Algerian women would unveil themselves, putting on the trappings of white European femininity, to avoid the suspicions of the French soldiers and pass through checkpoints in Algiers undetected. For Fanon, this form of cross-cultural performance was precisely *not* an identification but an imitation of one for political ends.

Nonetheless, when this scenario is directly staged *on film* – as in the pivotal scene from Gillo Pontecorvo's Third Cinema landmark, *The Battle of Algiers* (1966) – questions of identification return once more. Pontecorvo's film – a neorealist-style restaging of the struggle for Algerian independence – shows FLN operatives unveiling, cutting, and dying their hair, applying make-up, and donning Western clothes to distribute bombs throughout the city, as Fanon described. What the film adds to "Algeria Unveiled" is the logic of cinematic narrative, presenting the sequence as the women approach the checkpoints in the style of a suspense thriller. If we consider the scene in terms of Metz's secondary cinematic identification, then what we discover is the "vector" of identification that *The Battle of Algiers* offers to the spectator is an inversion of the one offered by *Tarzan*: by situating the story on the side of those fighting for independence from colonial rule, the film provides a place for its spectator – through use of close-ups and point-of-view – to associate with the FLN guerrillas, identify with them, even, as they plant bombs and assassinate occupiers (see Shohat & Stam [1994] 2014: 253). We might appreciate the radical political import of this cinematic identification if we were to imagine this scene's effect on a white European audience – certainly in a Parisian cinema of the 1960s (where *The Battle of Algiers* was banned upon release) but perhaps no less so today – that could find itself rooting *for* the colonised *against* the colonisers: in a sense, identifying against the empire of the self.

Such a destabilising encounter might have revolutionary potential, but if there can be a *politics* of identification, it can only be a profoundly ambivalent field. It would, necessarily, be something *other* than a politics of identity: identification problematises identity (understood as fixed essence) even while "it makes possible the formation of an *illusion* of identity as immediate, secure and totalizable" (Fuss, 1995: 2). It is a process of self-relation that leaves us open to change. As Metz and Fanon show, cinema presents a site for continual identifications. And even while seeing "oneself" represented on screen can have a transformative effect, cinematic identification does not depend on *likeness*. Psychoanalysis insists that identification entails not recognition but *misrecognition* of the self: the constitution of an "I" through an other.

As with *Tarzan* or *American Sniper*, this might be in relation to a specular ideal that, in a white supremacist/colonial context, has the capacity to encourage identification with the oppressor: turning spectatorship into a support for illusory ethnic/national "identity". But identification cuts both ways. Cinema also has the capacity to psychically align us with *anyone* or indeed anything: from a Calabrian fir tree to an Algerian freedom fighter. It can show us other worlds and other ideas, putting us in the shoes of those most *unlike* ourselves: whether that is a girl saving for a bicycle in Riyadh, as in Haifaa al-Mansour's *Wadjda* (2012), young women visited by the spirits of their drowned lovers in Mati Diop's *Atlantics* (2019) – itself a kind of spectral identification with the casualties of global capitalism (Fig. 2.2) – or a bourgeois Norfolk couple on the eve of their sapphire wedding anniversary in Andrew Haigh's *45 Years* (2015).

Yet, even here, there is a risk in the lure of a fantasy of total knowledge. Following Freud on oral incorporation, Fuss goes so far as to claim that identification itself operates according to a logic of *colonisation*: it is "an imperial process, a form of violent

Figure 2.2 Atlantics – Hauntings of global capital

appropriation in which the Other is deposed and assimilated into the lordly domain of the Self" (1995: 145). This leaves open the fundamental ethical problem of how to relate to an other without erasing their "otherness": a question that has exercised the philosophers from Confucius to Emmanuel Levinas, and to which psychoanalysis would bring the notion of *desire*. Cinematic identifications are never totalising: as Sobchack found, even the "primary" identification with the camera will meet its limit; while secondary identifications can be unpredictable, "mobile, elastic and volatile" (Fuss, 1995: 8) as they meet the enigma of the other's desire.

In this respect, McGowan's reading of *Lost in Translation* (2003) is instructive where he claims that it is in fact a more honest depiction of Japan from a Western perspective in its inability to find some sort of "authentic" experience beyond the surface (2016: 233–5). Sofia Coppola's film thus reveals – to paraphrase Žižek's "Hegelian witticism" about ancient Egypt – that *the mysteries of the Japanese were also the mysteries to the Japanese.*[5] As McGowan elsewhere expounds, this fundamentally anti-colonial understanding avoids "the racist trap of believing that the racial other somehow bypasses subjectivity and exists as a substantial entity, thereby harboring a secret knowledge" (2019: 189). From Tokyo to Riyadh to Norfolk, we might recognise the other on screen as a desiring subject like ourselves and identify, even momentarily, with their aims and struggles; but we must also recognise that, in the final analysis, their desire remains as opaque to them as it does to us. It is only from here that solidarity might be built.

Sympathy for the Devil

Fuss notes that, in the historical development of psychoanalysis, identification "replaces 'sympathy,' 'imagination,' and 'suggestion' to describe in a more 'scientific' fashion the phenomenon of how subjects act upon one another" (1995: 4); yet, in the consideration of how *cinema* acts upon its subjects, sympathy returns in what announces itself as a more "scientific" approach to film analysis. While there has been continual resistance to psychoanalysis in Film Studies (see Chapter 5), this peaked with the publication of David Bordwell and Noël Carroll's polemical *Post-Theory:*

Reconstructing Film Studies. This collection argued for a rejection of "Grand Theory" – "that aggregate of doctrines derived from Lacanian psychoanalysis, Structuralist semiotics, Post-Structuralist literary theory, and variants of Althusserian Marxism" (1996: xiii) – in favour of what they termed, rather unambitiously, "'middle-level' research" focusing on textual and historical analysis (27). This is characterised by Bordwell and Carroll as a marketplace of ideas, offering commonsense approaches on a case-by-case basis (xv).

Representative of this paradigm would be Murray Smith's cognitive film theory. Smith offers an alternative approach to the question of how we relate to screen media, based on spectatorship understood in terms of a "cognitive-anthropological model of mind" characterised by active problem-solving (1995: 9). In place of character identification, Smith introduces the "structure of sympathy" to describe how a cinemagoer forms bonds with those on screen. This begins, he suggests, with "recognition": picking out an individual character within the film and – with the understanding that they are nonetheless simply a collection of textual traits – comparing them to individuals, actions, values, etc. in the "real world". Next is alignment: "the process by which spectators are placed in relation to characters in terms of their access to their actions, and to what they know and feel" (83). We see and hear the things that they see and hear, and thereby gain insight into their thoughts and feelings. Smith calls the third stage "allegiance", which entails our moral evaluation and emotional response to a character, based on our alignment with them. Typically, by spending time with a character we develop an understanding of them. As Smith observes: "the conventional association of alignment and allegiance [...] primes us to be sympathetic to the characters with whom we are aligned" (188).

Smith explicitly situates his theory as engaging with the question of cinematic identification, and his tri-partite schema – recognition, alignment, allegiance – could be seen as a productive nuancing of those vectors of relation to character first put forward by Metz. The crucial difference is that Smith rejects the notion that we would *feel what the character feels* on screen as might be assumed in previous models of identification. Rather we feel *for* them: anxiety at their fear, rather than the fear itself. As Smith puts it:

> In sympathizing with the protagonist I do not simulate or mimic her occurrent mental state. Rather, I understand the protagonist and her context, make a more-or-less sympathetic or antipathetic judgment of the character, and respond emotionally in a manner appropriate to both the evaluation and the particular context of the action.
>
> (86)

What is striking is the tone of cool detachment here, in line with a cognitive "processing" model of spectatorship. I will leave it to the reader to determine whether Smith's account accurately reflects their own experience of watching a film, but what I will emphasise here are the limits or blind spots in Smith's formulation revealed by a psychoanalytic perspective.

Smith's reliance on *moral evaluation* as an explanation for "allegiance" – where he comes closest to secondary cinematic identification – raises important questions. Smith's insistence that "spectators construct moral structures, in which characters are organized and ranked in a system of preference" (84) assumes a *normative ethics*: i.e., we *should* be favourably disposed to morally "good" characters and not form similar attachments to morally "bad" characters. Nonetheless, the popularity of even genocidal villains such as Darth Vader and Thanos would seem to undermine this idea. Smith addresses this point in a later essay asking, "Just What Is It That Makes Tony Soprano Such An Appealing, Attractive Murderer?" (2011), which suggests that *The Sopranos* (1999–2007) presents its violent protagonist as a nonetheless likeable "regular guy" who remains morally superior to others in his world; while another cognitivist, Margrethe Bruun Vaage, argues that complex television series encourage our allegiance *despite* such immorality (2015).

Yet the fact that somebody else on screen might be deemed *worse*, from a moral perspective, than another character – a Gus Fring to a Walter White, a Ralph Cifaretto to a Tony Soprano – does not in itself account for the appeal of those figures who populate the "you missed the point by idolizing them" meme. The psychoanalytic perspective put forward by Adam Kotsko's *Why We Love Sociopaths* (2012) demonstrates that it is in fact *because* of their immorality that such characters are so compelling. For Kotsko, the screen "sociopath" – which covers all those characters identified at the start of this chapter – is another kind of specular ideal: the narcissistic fantasy of anti-social omnipotence. They offer a way out of the impasses of a "broken" late capitalist society. Sociopathic drama presents a vision of the world as "alienating and unjust, led by self-aggrandizing elites interested in (and competent at) little more than perpetuating their own power" (2012: 94). Those best suited to navigating a destructive and amoral society are themselves destructive and amoral: the schemers, climbers, and enforcers of contemporary screen media. Kotsko's sociopath gets ahead in life by ignoring, gaming, or otherwise instrumentalising social structures and expectations without being bound by them. The appeal of the screen sociopath is that of a position where our satisfactions are subject to no external limitation and we are beholden to no man.

This is particularly the case for someone as morally irredeemable as *American Psycho*'s (2000) mass-murdering finance bro, Patrick Bateman. The film's satirical commentary attempts to show how the material excesses of the hyper-capitalist 1980s might whither the human soul, but – for a certain audience – this is simply eclipsed by the outpouring of imagined *enjoyment* (see Chapters 4 and 5) that Bateman embodies. He is taken as an image of the subject undivided and unlimited. Despite his unpalatable features, *and even his framing within the film as a pathetic and deluded character*, he has become an online face of the "sigma grindset", a hyperbolic valorisation of ruthless competition, violent egotism, and misogyny that finds its way from Reddit and TikTok to the spectacle of the US presidency.

Jason Mittell, another cognitivist, characterises those audiences who, for example, celebrate rather than condemn Walter White – precisely the target of the "starter pack" meme – as "bad fans" (2022), again suggesting the imposition of a normative ethics: they are not responding to the screen as they *should* do. But such a reading is as impotent in the field of screen analysis as it has proven in the field of political analysis. Kotsko demonstrates that such fans are responding precisely as they are being *permitted* to respond by the sociopath's performance of unlimited satisfaction. The foreclosure of desire in cognitive film theory shows the "common sense" of middle-level research to be apolitical and regressive: undone by the "nonsense" of the unconscious. Just as the 2008 financial crisis revealed the economic marketplace to be driven by self-destructive "irrationality", and global populist political campaigns have demonstrated the compelling force of reactionary enjoyment, so too is the marketplace of ideas proffered by "post-theory" undermined by its denial of irrational responses to the screen. There can be no purchase on the problems we face without acknowledging the perspective of psychoanalysis.

Before we abandon identification entirely, however, there remains a further possibility in what Žižek calls the "over-orthodox" position: radical identification with the dominant values – taking the social order more seriously than it takes itself – to undermine it from within (1997b: 58). Žižek states that the Law requires certain, permitted "inherent transgressions" – like driving over the speed limit or cheating on one's taxes – to support its normal functioning, by giving a sense that we are not fully grasped by its ideological system. An over-orthodox identification refuses such unspoken understanding and insists steadfastly on taking the system at face value, thus collapsing the distance between Law and its negation.[6] This is demonstrated in Yorgos Lanthimos' *Dogtooth* (2009), where the controlling patriarch constructs a mythology to keep his adult children within the confines of the family compound: telling them that the world outside is a dangerous place that they will be ready to face only when they have shed their canine teeth and regrown another set. He is permitted to leave thanks to the protection of his Mercedes, while they will simply have to wait. Of course, the children are unwittingly trapped because, at their age, they cannot expect any more teeth to grow. Nonetheless, the eldest daughter plots her escape through radical over-identification: taking the paternal regime more seriously than it is prepared to take itself, she bashes out her canine teeth and climbs covertly inside the boot of the family car. While her fate remains unknown, her disappearance causes a catastrophic breakdown in the social structure while leaving open the possibility of future freedom.[7] These are ideas we will explore in Chapters 4 and 5. For now, we must move on, turning to *the* decisive moment for psychoanalytic film theory and everything that was to follow: in the question of sexual difference.

Notes

1 The meme has been reworked to include Bojack Horseman, Rustin Cohle (*True Detective*), "D-Fens" (*Falling Down*), The Punisher (Marvel), and Homelander (*The Boys*); adapted to a "GirlBoss Edition" featuring Daenerys Targaryen and Harley Quinn; and a version made up solely of pictures of Hegel. See: https://knowyourmeme.com/memes/the-you-missed-the-point-by-idolizing-them-starter-pack
2 Vicky Lebeau notes that the mirror was also a foundational metaphor for psychoanalysis itself, with Freud advising analysts to be "like a mirror … show[ing the analysand] nothing but what is shown to him" (quoted in Lebeau, 2014: 172).
3 Patrick Fuery, conversely, argues that this is precisely what happens in the cinema. He characterises spectatorship as *madness*: entry into a world of Lacanian psychotic delusion, hallucination, and paranoia, where everything becomes potentially meaningful (2003: 70–98).
4 Pietro Bianchi's *Jacques Lacan and Cinema* (2017) also offers an alternative philosophical approach to questions of perception and ideology from a Lacanian perspective, reaching beyond the early theories of the mirror stage.
5 Žižek summarises Hegel's discussion, in his lectures on *Aesthetics*, of the seemingly unsolvable puzzles of Egyptian art, noting: "the secrets of the Egyptians were secrets also for the Egyptians" (2012a: 477).
6 Žižek points to Ayn Rand as someone who took American capitalism more seriously than it takes itself and thus laid bare its ruthless, asocial logic (2017: 98).
7 For an extended Lacanian reading of *Dogtooth*, see Tyrer (2017).

Chapter 3

Difference

Writing in the Autumn 1975 issue of that British film journal, Laura Mulvey noted: "Recent writing in *Screen* about psychoanalysis and the cinema has not sufficiently brought out the importance of the representation of the female form in a symbolic order in which, in the last resort, it speaks castration and nothing else" (1975: 6). This observation, of course, comes from the second paragraph of "Visual Pleasure and Narrative Cinema": perhaps the most famous essay in Anglophone Film Studies. First drafted in 1973, its arguments are now so embedded in popular discourse that contemporary filmmakers such as Joanna Hogg and Todd Haynes will cite its influence, and it can be referenced not once but twice on popular US TV sitcom *Parks and Recreation* (2009–2015). There is certainly a lot to unpack in those 39 words quoted above, and very many more words have subsequently been written in response: particularly in the context of feminist film theory and wider cultural analysis. It would be beyond the capacity of this book to present an overview of the entire field of debate that has developed in the ensuing five decades, and so I will focus on the particularly psychoanalytic dimensions of Mulvey's argument and limit attention in this chapter to some key responses to her work.[1]

Mulvey's own aims become apparent in the opening to her essay: the previous issue of *Screen* had presented an English translation of Metz's "The Imaginary Signifier", and whether or not "recent writing" is alluding to this piece in particular, it is clear that Mulvey has the paradigm of Apparatus theory – with its effaced, sexless, quasi-universal spectator – in her sights here. More broadly, as an active member of the Women's Liberation Movement and a film theorist, Mulvey takes as her target the conventional representations of women in visual culture from Western art history to advertising and screen media that, as John Berger had observed, address "the [male] spectator-owner looking at it" as the "sexual protagonist" of the scene (1972: 56).

Mulvey's basic contention is that psychoanalytic film theory had not paid sufficient attention to the question of *sexual difference*. This chapter will, therefore, look at how psychoanalytic film theory has attempted to account for difference in the cinematic encounter. This will entail reappraisal of Mulvey's theory of the "male gaze" and its implications for our understanding of gender and sexuality on screen. But this will also entail consideration of their intersections with race and ethnicity, building on those insights from postcolonial and critical race theory introduced in the previous chapter, before concluding with some reflections on how such interactions might point us in new directions for psychoanalytic film thinking and questions of "white visual pleasure".

A Political Use of Psychoanalysis

To understand Mulvey's argument, it is important to recognise her as a feminist critic writing in the 1970s and looking back at the Hollywood cinema of the 1940s and '50s with a mixture of appreciation and dismay. The essay can be seen as an attempt to work through a contradiction in her own experience as, on the one hand, an ardent fan of classical Hollywood and, on the other, a strident critic of its sexist representations.

The first section bears the heading "A political use of psychoanalysis", aligning it with both the turn towards Freud and Lacan in the feminist work of Juliet Mitchell (1974) and the turn towards politics in 1970s film theory (see Chapter 5). "In a world", as Mulvey puts it, "ordered by sexual imbalance" (1975: 11) – i.e., founded on a fundamental inequality between women and men – psychoanalysis offered a framework for understanding, even *diagnosing*, the social order as it was determined by the law of the father so it could then be dismantled in the interests of an emancipatory politics. Freud and

Lacan's theories can be understood as attempts to account for how sexual difference is made manifest both bodily and socially. This framework Mulvey turned towards the analysis of film, declaring: "Psychoanalytic theory is thus appropriate here as a political weapon, demonstrating the way the unconscious of patriarchal society has structured film form" (1975: 6). Hollywood cinema, as the hegemonic Western cultural practice, was determined by the prevailing patriarchal ideology, which could be described precisely in psychoanalytic terms.

Echoing the famous thesis put forward by Simone de Beauvoir ([1949] 2011) – that woman is the "other sex", giving man his identity through her difference – Mulvey observed:

> Woman then stands in patriarchal culture as signifier for the male other, bound by a symbolic order in which man can live out his phantasies and obsessions through linguistic command by imposing them on the silent image of woman still tied to her place as bearer of meaning, not maker of meaning.
>
> (1975: 6)

Patriarchal ideology structures film form and, by extension, the formation of subjectivity through spectatorship: woman is both what does not "fit" *and* what helps maintain the (male) subject's imaginary unity. In response, Mulvey calls – and this is sometimes overlooked in the essay – for alternative filmmaking practices that fight the positioning of woman as silent image: by *destroying visual pleasure* with a feminist counter-cinema aesthetic. Mulvey and her partner Peter Wollen put theory into practice through avant-garde work such as *Riddles of the Sphinx* (1977), which used overt theoretical discussion and self-reflexive camerawork – such as long, 360-degree panning shots – to reflect on the intersections of class and gender in British society; but it would be another landmark work of 1975 – Chantal Akerman's *Jeanne Dielman, 23 quai du Commerce, 1080 Bruxelles*, which Mulvey recalls seeing at an impactful Edinburgh Film Festival screening – that would make an indelible mark on the cinematic aesthetics and politics of sexual difference, through its rigorous formal examination of the unravelling life of Delphine Seyrig's inscrutable Belgian housewife.

The Male Gaze

While *Jeanne Dielman* is vitally important to cinema history – and was eventually voted *Sight and Sound* "Greatest Film of All Time" in 2022 – it remains the exception more than the rule when it comes to representations of women on screen, which have tended far more towards heteropatriarchal conventions. This takes us, then, into the realm of what Mulvey called the "male gaze": a term that, as noted above, has entered popular parlance as a shorthand for misogyny in visual culture, while also – as we will see in the next chapter – opening the way for significant *misinterpretations* of the relationship between cinema and psychoanalysis.[2] Nonetheless, according to Mulvey we should recognise that films are shaped by masculine fantasies of woman because this is how the society in which they are produced is itself shaped. Classical Hollywood cinema is organised according to a visual logic that conforms to and supports (traditional, heterosexual) men's desires. This *masculine* visual regime is what she christens the "male gaze". Mulvey observes that, under this order, "pleasure in looking has been split between active/male and passive/female. The determining male gaze projects its fantasy onto the female figure, which is styled accordingly" (1975: 7). Men are presented on screen as "active", taking pleasure in looking; while women are presented as "passive", objects *to be looked at*.

The chief appeal of narrative cinema is that it offers us *pleasure in looking* (or what Freud called "scopophilia"). This visual pleasure functions in two modes: *narcissism* and *voyeurism*. Narcissism, or pleasure in looking at myself, relates to Lacan's theory of the mirror stage and fantasies of potency, as discussed by Baudry and Metz in the previous chapter. This is aligned with an idealised image of an active individual: the male hero, who drives the narrative forward. At the same time, it is also dependent on voyeurism, or pleasure in looking at others. This relies on anonymity and distance: precisely the environment offered by the darkened cinema auditorium. Voyeurism requires a passive object who serves as erotic spectacle: the female lead, who functions purely as image. What Mulvey identifies as the "male gaze" is therefore the way in which cinema creates a *position for the spectator* through narcissism and voyeurism that assumes/reproduces a (traditional, heterosexual) masculine identity irrespective of their own identity/ embodiment.

Like Baudry and Metz, Mulvey takes up ideas of identification but introduces a question of sexual difference absent from the mirror stage. Mulvey recognises cinematic identification as (mis) recognition of a character who is "like me" or perhaps "how I would like to be" and notes that idealised images of movie stars offer ample sources of such attraction for the spectator. In classical Hollywood, this identification is typically made with the film's male hero. The spectator's relation to him is *not* one of objectification: the hero is not made erotic spectacle. Instead, he functions as that "ideal ego" of masculinity: the more powerful, more perfect one that I could (never) be like. Think Bogart and Mitchum, then; or more recently, Pitt and Gosling. He is presented as commanding the stage: he is the figure who drives the narrative forward as a vehicle for the spectator's identity.

This narcissism is supported by both the apparatus of the cinema itself and the visual logic of classical Hollywood. Not unlike Metz, Mulvey identifies different "looks" in the relay of spectatorship – that of the camera, the character within the diegesis, and the spectator before the screen – all of which align with man as the "bearer of the look" (i.e., the one who is looking) under the logic of the "male gaze" (11). The spectator is encouraged to look at the male protagonist – not as object, but as ideal – and thereby to look where he looks and to what he looks at, which is woman. Mulvey cites Lauren Bacall in *To Have and Have Not* (1944) as paradigmatic of woman's cinematic function as erotic object for both character and spectator: as in the famous bar scene, where we watch with the camera, watching Bogart, watching "Slim" (Bacall) as she keeps the whole room in rapt attention.

Mulvey highlights the gendered dynamics of what Metz called "primary cinematic identification" with the camera. Classical cinema requires narcissistic identification with the hero to access the mode of voyeurism offered by the film. As Metz observed, the visual regime of cinema depends upon the absence of the object seen. We see its replica, its representation rather than the object itself. Cinema, Mulvey notes, thus allows for observation at a safe distance in the mode of the Peeping Tom. It is a pleasure driven by our curiosity about other people and grounded ultimately, Freud suggested, in the fantasy of the "primal scene": a moment where the child witnesses (or imagines) their parents having sex (SE 17: 29). The spectator is thus like a little kid peering through the keyhole into mum and dad's bedroom, giving us another psychoanalytic metaphor for film theory: *cinema as peep hole*.

In a classic Freudian reversal, however, Mulvey notes:

> Although the film is really being shown, is there to be seen, conditions of screening and narrative conventions give the spectator an illusion of looking in on a private world. Among other things, the position of the spectators in the cinema is blatantly one of repression of their exhibitionism and projection of the repressed desire onto the performer.
> (1975: 9)

Our pleasure in looking at others is really an inverted form of our pleasure in *being looked at*, which can be successfully repressed in the dark space of the cinema. The contract of spectatorship is based on *exhibitionism* rather than voyeurism, as we might expect: exhibitionism enacted but disavowed on screen (the film invites us to look at it, but in such a way that it allows us to believe we are catching it unawares); and exhibitionism repressed, reversed into voyeurism (the cinematic invitation to look addresses our own unconscious desire *to be seen*).

These libidinal dynamics are laid bare in David Lynch's *Blue Velvet* (1986): when Jeffrey Beaumont peers out of the closet as Dorothy undresses, this scene reproduces the classical understanding of spectatorship in terms of the stolen thrill of *voyeurism*; yet, when Dorothy discovers Jeffrey and forces him to strip at knife point, this violent humiliation embodies the true, unconscious satisfaction of *being seen* that is made available in the cinematic encounter. Moreover, when Frank arrives and Jeffrey is forced back into the closet, Dorothy continues her "performance" in full knowledge that she is being watched: reminding us again of the exhibitionist pact upon which cinema is predicated. We experience cinema as a fantasy of violation of the other to guard against the enjoyment of our own vulnerability. Where Baudry might have recognised Ana Torrent as the paradigmatic, child-like spectator of the dream-cave, for Mulvey we are instead much closer to the ingénue-pervert-detective of Lynchian nightmare.

Nonetheless, the voyeuristic visual logic of cinema is reinforced by the construction of woman in classical Hollywood. She is presented as pure image: source of visual pleasure for the hero and by extension the spectator. She is the object of desire that provokes the hero and thus the narrative. Mulvey observes:

> [Women's appearance] is coded for strong visual and erotic impact so that they can be said to connote to-be-looked-at-ness. Woman displayed as sexual object is the leitmotif of erotic spectacle: from pin-ups to striptease [...] she holds the look, and plays to and signifies male desire.
>
> (11)

Woman is thus moulded to the contours of masculine fantasy, and this functions in a reciprocal way to support the logic of the "male gaze": the image of woman is styled to invite us to look at her, placing the spectator in the masculine position. As a function of the patriarchal unconscious, Hollywood cinema is determined by (traditional, heterosexual) male desire and its mode of spectatorship is *masculine by default*.

If the spectator in Hollywood cinema is encouraged to identify narcissistically with the hero of the film, and women are presented on screen as objects to-be-looked-at for visual pleasure, then the locus classicus here would of course be the famous Ernie's restaurant scene from *Vertigo* (1958), where Madeleine's emerald green dress is designed to scream "Look at me!" against the ruby red walls of the dining room: she is pure spectacle for Scottie and spectator alike. This logic also persists in contemporary visual culture with, for example, the striking technique used by travel companies and tourist boards of an advertisement shot in first person POV, looking at a conventionally attractive woman (styled to-be-looked-at). A masculine arm enters the bottom of the frame, she takes "his" hand and guides us through the sights of the holiday destination. The message is clear: she stands for the exotic delights of distant lands and a promise of pleasure; "he" is merely an empty vessel, a container for the masculinised spectator who will, presumably, be purchasing this attractive holiday as Berger's *sexual protagonist* of the scene.

Yet Mulvey also notes a tension in the organisation of the "male gaze", between narrative and spectacle:

> The presence of woman is an indispensable element of spectacle in a normal narrative film, yet her visual presence tends to work against the development of a story line, to freeze the flow of action in moments of erotic contemplation.
>
> (11)

Woman is made to perform as image to ensure the cohesion of masculine identity and the flow of the film, but she hinders them as well. Again, *Vertigo* is exemplary here: as Madeleine passes by Scottie in the restaurant, everything stops as she is framed in close-up for the spectator's contemplation. And again, we see these techniques persisting today, as in the presentation of Megan Fox's Mikaela as sex object in *Transformers* (2007). In Michael Bay's film, Sam's intelligent robot-car intentionally breaks down to contrive a meet-cute between the characters: their journey and the film alike coming to a halt at this point to linger on her body (Fig. 3.1).

This conflict between movement and stasis points us in the direction of a fundamental *contradiction* for Mulvey in the logic of

Figure 3.1 Transformers – Halting the narrative

the male gaze: looking at woman is not just a source of visual pleasure. She is also troubling, a source of potential *unpleasure*. The spectacle of the woman's body evokes the threat of *castration*. She is, in Mulvey's colourful phrase, "bearer of the bleeding wound" (7): a reminder of the loss (symbolic for Lacan, more literal for Freud) that haunts the masculine psyche. To allay castration anxiety, film offers the patriarchal unconscious two avenues of escape: *fetishism* and *sadism*. For Mulvey, "fetishistic scopophilia" entails an obsessive fascination with the image of woman. This recalls Freud's (SE 21: 155) idea of the crucial fetish object in perversion – as the thing which distracts us, allows us to *disavow* castration – and manifests here as the over-valuation of the woman's image. In aesthetic terms, this is associated with the cinematic *close-up*: the camera breaks woman up into discrete images, reducing her to a collection of body parts, with the overwhelming beauty of these objects offering a distraction from anxiety. The other, Mulvey suggests, is to punish the woman through voyeurism, which always involves an element of sadism. First by investigating her allure to demystify or dispel it and then destroying or punishing her as a guilty object: as in narratives containing her through marriage or simply killing her off. Comedies conventionally end with the former – e.g., independent, forthright Hildy is re-married to Walter at the end of *His Girl Friday* (1940) – while thrillers frequently end with the latter. Paradigmatic here is the noir femme fatale, who is subjected to both fetishistic scopophilia *and* sadistic voyeurism. *Double Indemnity*'s (1944) Phyllis Dietrichson, for instance, is introduced to us wearing only a towel and descending a staircase to draw attention to what Neff calls "that honey of an anklet": an object that stands in metonymically-fetishistically for her whole body. By the end of the film, their relationship has collapsed, and she is shot by Neff: her scheme to emancipate herself from patriarchal strictures (by murdering her wealthy husband) is punished by death.

In subsequent decades, debates will rage as to what degree of agency figures such as Hildy and Phyllis in fact achieved, whether the "male gaze" gives a satisfactory account of the sexual politics of spectatorship, and, in fact, whether Mulvey's essay even constitutes a properly *psychoanalytic* engagement with cinema. There are also important counter-examples in film history, such as the trailblazing work of Alice Guy or Ida Lupino, and perhaps most strikingly Dorothy Arzner's *Dance, Girl, Dance* (1940), which includes a remarkable scene where protagonist Judy O'Brien halts her performance at a burlesque show to upbraid the mostly male audience for "staring at a girl the way your wives won't let you"; while even the examples from Hitchcock are not necessarily as straightforward as they first seem (see Chapter 4). Nonetheless, as a diagnosis of the sexism at the heart of mainstream visual culture, and in Hollywood film aesthetics specifically, "Visual Pleasure and Narrative Cinema" remains a valuable touchstone.

"Afterthoughts" and After

Responses to "Visual Pleasure and Narrative Cinema" have been wide-ranging, including Mulvey's own "Afterthoughts on 'Visual Pleasure and Narrative Cinema' inspired by King Vidor's *Duel in the Sun* (1946)".[3] She notes facing "the persistent question 'what about the women in the audience?'" as a point of departure for this latter essay. Mulvey offers a useful clarification, explaining that she was interested in "the relationship between the image of woman on the screen and the 'masculinisation' of the spectator position, regardless of the actual sex [...] of any real live moviegoer" (1981: 12). The theory of the "male gaze" is not necessarily about *men* looking in/at films but about *the construction of the film image according to a logic we might describe as masculine*: how classical cinema offers a point of view often associated with (traditional, heterosexual) masculinity, in fact, to *any* spectator.

Mulvey suggests that this construction might be a barrier to women in the audience, who "may find herself so out of key with the pleasure on offer, with its masculinisation, that the spell of fascination is broken" (12); alternatively, she might appreciate adopting the *masculine position* and take up the pleasures of identifying with the active male protagonist. Mulvey references Freud's theory of femininity to suggest that women are capable of such a "trans-sex identification" (13), and that even where there is a female protagonist in the film there remains an element of "tomboy" masculinity for the woman. In either case, however, the woman "does not sit easily and shifts restlessly in [her] borrowed transvestite clothes [because] the female spectator's fantasy of masculinisation [is] at cross-purposes with itself" (15). Mulvey's archaic use of language notwithstanding, her point is that although adoption of a masculine perspective can be liberating for the female spectator, it is only a temporary act of role-play often leading to further problems of understanding and enjoyment for the woman in front of the screen. There is no genuine (feminine) subjectivity, just a temporary fantasy of masculinisation.

Mary Ann Doane takes up these considerations in her own analysis of cinematic femininity and "masquerade". Again, the question for Doane is the relation between woman and screen, and again she finds classical cinema to offer an ambivalent space of identifications. Doane suggests several possibilities here: the first is "transvestitism" (1982: 80), echoing both Mulvey's outmoded terminology and the idea of adopting a masculine position through images of man on screen. In relation to images of women, Doane offers "masochistic over-identification" with the image, "the narcissism entailed in becoming one's own object of desire", or, alternatively, taking up the *masquerade* of femininity (87). For Doane, the female spectator is not afforded distance from the image because it is so like her own; rather than taking up a position of "fetishism" (as Metz/Mulvey suggested), however, she engages with it *directly*. This risks masochistic entrapment in over-identifying with the woman on screen (for Doane much less radical than for Žižek because the spectator simply reacts *as if the film were happening to her*), or collapse into narcissistic objectification before the spectacle of woman: effectively becoming the object of her own desire.

If femininity is constructed as over-closeness to the image, then the way out for Doane entails establishing a degree of critical distance from the screen. Building on Joan Riviere's clinical paper, "Womanliness as Masquerade" (1929) – in which Riviere discussed women who perform an exaggerated display of femininity to deflect male hostility – Doane notes that

> The masquerade, in flaunting femininity, holds it at a distance. 'Womanliness' is a mask which can be worn or removed. [...] By destabilising the image, the masquerade

confounds this masculine structure of the look. It effects a defamiliarisation of female iconography.

(1982: 81–2)

Many decades before Judith Butler's intervention (1990), Riviere showed that femininity was not innate but *performed*, a mask to be put on or taken off. For Doane, this meant that images of femininity on screen could equally be "manipulable, producible, and readable by the woman" (1982: 87). Such an understanding might allow us to subvert even regressive images of woman. This could put us in the bind of Rita Hayworth's Gilda, who is able to use the excessive performance of femininity in the striptease to control the men around her while remaining within the confines of a patriarchal structure; or it could point to other, more emancipatory possibilities. Nonetheless, while subsequent debates and trends in visual culture have looked for agency in overt portrayals of female sexuality – see, for example, Megan Fox again in the ironically self-aware *Jennifer's Body* (2009) – critics of a "post-feminist" tendency have also asked why "empowerment" in mainstream culture still so often resembles masculine fantasy (e.g., Gill, 2006).

The Female Gaze

Where Mulvey, Doane, and Cowie (1997) noted that the genre of melodrama opened spaces in classical cinema for interrogation of women's experiences on screen – and were also among the critics who addressed the topic of feminist filmmaking practice – more recent attention has turned to the specific question of a "female gaze" in film. As Erika Balsom (2020) observes, there is still confusion around this term: sometimes it is associated simply with films made by women, or with films that women tend to view. The French film critic Iris Brey offers a new approach in *Le regard féminin: Une révolution à l'écran* (*The Female Gaze: A Revolution on Screen*, not yet translated into English). For Brey, the "female gaze" – a term she uses in English to emphasise dialogue with Mulvey and psychoanalytic film theory – is less about who is watching (as it had been for Doane) than the qualities of the film itself. *Le regard féminin* sets out six key features characterising the female gaze. It involves a narrative in which "the main character identifies as a woman", it is "told from her point of view", and it "challenges the patriarchal order"; and in terms of film language, it stages "the female experience" through mise-en-scène, it deploys eroticism as a conscious gesture because "Laura Mulvey reminds us that the *male gaze* stems from the patriarchal unconscious", and its pleasure "does not derive from a scopic drive (taking pleasure in looking at a person by objectifying them, like a voyeur)".[4] Brey reflects that this framework could function "like the Bechdel test used to highlight […] the under-representation of female characters on screen" (2020: 77) but goes beyond that paradigm in emphasising the role of film form as well as narrative/dialogue: i.e., not just *who* is represented on screen but crucially *how* they are represented, too.

The key example of this logic for Brey is Céline Sciamma's *Portrait of a Lady on Fire* (2019), which presents a filmic reflection on the dynamics of the "gaze" and a bold redefinition of the language of cinematic desire: "no longer built on asymmetry but on the principle of equality" (2020: 217). The story of an artist, Marianne, sent to paint a portrait of aristocratic daughter Héloïse without the latter's knowledge, *Portrait of a Lady on Fire* begins with the principles of the male gaze as Mulvey and Berger had defined them: the painter looks at her model through the cinematic point-of-view structure, aligning Marianne with the activity of the camera and Héloïse with the apparent passivity of the object of fascination, each on either side of the shot/reverse-shot pattern. Yet, in a crucial scene at the centre of the film, Héloïse reminds Marianne that for as long as the artist has been looking at her, she has been looking right back. Rather than a subject/object relation, this has always been the meeting of two desiring subjects: a dynamic expressed filmically by the shift from singles (i.e., each character framed alone within the scene) to the two-shot, putting both characters on equal footing within the same frame (Fig. 3.2).[5] As Brey observes, "We leave behind a relationship of domination to explore the development of desire horizontally" (2020: 217), not abandoning the realms of visual pleasure entirely – *Portrait of a Lady on Fire* is an exceptionally beautiful film – but finding new ways to express sexuality and embodiment on screen.

Figure 3.2 Portrait of a Lady on Fire – Horizonal desire

Balsom suggests that Brey's cinema of the female gaze would seem to preclude voyeurism and objectification of any kind: the ogling of men's bodies in *Magic Mike XXL* (2015), for example, presenting the same hierarchical logic as Mulvey's male gaze with men and women merely changing places (Balsom, 2020). And while, as Balsom notes, Brey's female gaze is, in one respect, explicitly trans-inclusive and overtly feminist in its politics, it also excludes films about men (and potentially intersex and non-binary people), even where they would similarly suggest new visual logics and circuits of desire: such as Claire Denis' *Beau Travail* (1999), Lucía Puenzo's *XXY* (2007), or even Sciamma's *Tomboy* (2011). Brey also does not seem to acknowledge the extent to which *Portrait of a Lady on Fire* constitutes a *queering* of the "gaze" in its exploration of passion between two women; while critics such as Clara Bradbury-Rance (2022) and Susan Potter (2022) have shown how Sciamma's film makes sex visible *differently*, without relying on the tendency towards explicit representation common in contemporary European cinema (e.g., Abdellatif Kechiche's adaptation of *Blue is the Warmest Colour* [2013], very much a film of the "male gaze"). Writing contemporaneously to Brey and also offering vital reflections on Sciamma, Kelli Fuery sets out a more theoretically rigorous distinction between these visual logics: putting forward concepts of the "imperialist" and "reciprocal" gazes in cinema (2022: 221). Informed by psychoanalysis and the phenomenology of Beauvoir, Fuery's *Ambiguous Cinema* lays bare the filmic and psychic mechanisms at work for Mulvey and for Brey, even while decoupling the concepts from their apparently gendered specificity.

Masculinity and Visual Pleasure

Steve Neale also writes in response to "Visual Pleasure", considering what happens when the "male gaze" meets *masculinity* on screen in ways that both extend and challenge Mulvey's thinking. He concurs with Mulvey (and Apparatus theory) that looking is a vehicle for *identification* in classical cinema, and that the masculine image offers a "powerful ideal ego" (1983: 5) for the spectator (that more perfect "mirror image" of the narcissistic fantasy). Drawing on the work of Raymond Bellour and Mulvey's "Afterthoughts", Neale characterises this in terms of the Oedipal trajectory of conventional narratives reproducing traditional, heterosexual masculinity as the "structuring norm" (2). Bellour identified the Oedipal myth as it determined masculinity in *North By Northwest* (1959), for example: charting Roger Thornhill's development from, as Neale summarises, "infantile dependence on the mother to a position of 'adult', 'male', heterosexual masculinity, sealed by his marriage" (4), as Thornhill encounters the *princess* (Eva), vanquishes the *bad father* (Vandamm), and supersedes the *good father* (The Professor) by becoming the *husband*. This passage from boy to man to father thanks to the love of a good woman functions as a regulating ideal, giving expression to what Lee Edelman calls the social order's "compulsory narrative of reproductive futurism" (2004: 21).

Neale takes Bellour further, noting that the classical narrative of masculine identity turns on a "contradiction between narcissism and the Law" (1983: 9). Drawing again on Mulvey's "Afterthoughts", he identifies a tension between "an image of narcissistic authority on the one hand and the image of social authority on the other" (9). Narcissistic masculinity "involve[s] phantasies of power, omnipotence, mastery and control" (5), based on a nostalgia for that pre-Oedipal infantile state where the child enjoyed an imagined sense of potency in the blurring of inner and outer worlds. Social masculinity, by contrast, involves acquiescence to the Oedipal narrative: taking one's place in society through the structure of the family. With Mulvey, Neale finds these "two diverging images of masculinity commonly at play in the Western" (9), particularly in *The Man Who Shot Liberty Valance* (1962): John Wayne's Tom Doniphon represents the "old ways" – a seemingly omnipotent, mythical individual – and while James Stewart's Ransom Stoddard is tempted by this path, he ultimately settles into his career as a lawyer and politician and marries the love-interest, Hallie. The film suggests the necessity of this socialising, Oedipal trajectory but – in being structured around Doniphon's funeral – still retains a mournful yearning for the narcissistic path.

This type of "choice" between regressive and progressive forms of masculinity is common in film narrative, from Chief Brody between Quint (past) and Hooper (future) in *Jaws* (1975), to – as we will see in Chapter 5 – the choice between Steve Lift's reactionary, individualised *billionaire masculinity* and the *radical, social masculinity* of the protagonist's working-class peers in *Sorry to Bother You* (2018). Relating back to the structures of identification described in Chapter 2, we can first see at work a "tertiary" (or intra-diegetic) level of cinematic identification – the protagonist must choose one of the paths for his life, narcissism or society – followed, potentially, by the "secondary" level as the same choice is offered to the spectator, who might yet reject the family and invest in the nostalgic images of the "John Wayne" mythology. As we saw, the pull of this anti-social narcissism remains strong, explaining everything from the popularity of "first person shooter" video games to the late career resurgence of Liam Neeson as a violent action hero.

In such instances, the image of the man on screen functions as a powerful ideal: just like the infant's reflection in the mirror, it seems better, more potent and thus preferable as a model for the ego. Neale, however, notes a contradiction in this process:

> While the ideal ego may be a 'model' with which the subject identifies and to which it aspires, it may also be a source of further images and feelings of castration, inasmuch as that ideal is something to which the subject is never adequate.
>
> (7)

Where Mulvey suggested that woman evokes castration by embodying symbolic lack, Neale suggests that idealised images of men can also be threatening for the masculine ego by embodying *potency*, leading to feelings of inadequacy and the encounter with lack once more. Masculinity in mainstream visual culture thus remains an impossible ideal.

Yet, the masculine is not just a vehicle for identification: it can also function as *spectacle* in a way not considered by Mulvey, for whom to-be-looked-at-ness is necessarily feminine. Neale asserts that male figures on screen can also be the object of voyeuristic looking. In certain classical narrative situations – e.g., traditionally masculine genres such as the war film and gangster movie – a battle for supremacy between men gives screen time to male bodies. Violence and competition thus become a cover, an excuse for looking at men, even allowing for a fetishistic fascination with the male form. In contemporary context, we need only think of the many fight scenes in high octane action movies such as the *Fast and Furious* franchise, where encounters between Vin Diesel, Dwayne Johnson, and Jason Momoa afford us numerous shots of their hard-body physiques, with lingering close-ups on faces, arms, and hands staging a spectacular masculine imaginary.

Neale also identifies a further tension in this presentation of *masculinity as a source of visual pleasure*. If the classical film is constructed according to the heteropatriarchal logic of the "male gaze", then the *erotic* dimension of masculine spectacle is a *problem* that must be suppressed: the *masculinised spectator* should not be presented with a masculine sex object. Homoeroticism cannot be directly avowed and will be avoided, Neale suggests, either by putting the man in a "feminised" position, or through sadomasochistic fantasies of the male body's destruction. Neale points briefly to Rock Hudson's presentation in the melodrama of Douglas Sirk as an explicit "object of an erotic look", which, he observes, "is usually marked as female" (14). Neale seems to assume that simply being rendered a sex object is enough for Hudson to be "feminised", but if we take *All that Heaven Allows* (1955) as a key example here, then the situation is more nuanced. The camera certainly lingers on Ron's (Hudson) burly frame and marvels at his connection to nature, presenting this spectacle in terms of the heroine Cary's attraction to him. Yet it seems counterintuitive to argue that Ron would be *feminised* by this overtly heterosexual circuit of desire. The more conventional "feminisation" of Ron would come towards the film's end, where, after an accident, he is rendered *passive*: prostrate on Cary's couch to be nursed back to health. His sexual potency is reduced, and potential homoeroticism (for the masculinised spectator) diverted.

Ron's fate thus points us towards Neale's other avenue of escape for the masculine ego: *destruction* of the male body as source of visual pleasure. Voyeurism, as we saw, involves an element of sadism – e.g., punishment of the woman – but there must also be an element of *masochism* here, too: to see the masculine mirror image punished is to see "myself" (as masculinised spectator) punished. Here Neale references Paul Willemen's analysis of Anthony Mann's noir films, where a protagonist must look on helplessly as his friend or partner is beaten or killed: the potent male body both on display and repressed by the film. In contemporary cinema, we find both tendencies condensed in the Daniel Craig iteration of James Bond, which stages these fantasies in particularly vivid terms, both supporting and complicating Neale's assertions. In an early scene from *Casino Royale* (2006), Bond emerges from the waves in a self-conscious evocation of Ursula Andress' introduction in the first Bond film, *Dr No* (1962). As Honey Ryder steps out of the Caribbean Sea, she sets the tone for the "Bond Girl" as source of visual pleasure throughout the franchise and so, in 2006, Bond is literally in the *woman's position* within the frame. But can this really be considered a "feminisation"? Instead, it should be seen as hypermasculine display. Here he is not invalided like Hudson but active and virile, a potential source of visual pleasure *and* narcissistic identification at the same time; and not in the so-called "women's genre" of melodrama but in the contemporary action-adventure movie.

Moreover, in a startling scene towards the end of the film, Bond is captured by the villain, Le Chiffre, who has him bound to a chair. Bond is stripped bare – every sinew and muscle there to see in fetishistic close-up and lingering long shot – while he is counterbalanced by the fully-clothed Le Chiffre. The homoerotic element is more directly acknowledged than in classical cinema: Le Chiffre admires the spectacle of Bond, commenting "You've taken good care of your body ...", although this ultimately diverts queerness onto the figure of the villain, containing or defusing its potential once more. Bond's pumped-up, "phallic" masculinity is both on display and repressed by the film: we can look but only as long as his masculinity is *ruined*, as Le Chiffre beats him – violently destroying his "manhood" (i.e., genitals) – with a large rope (Fig. 3.3).

Marginal Masculinities

Casino Royale seems to reproduce those conventional fantasies described by Neale and Willemen but in showing the *aftermath* of violence also points to alternative possibilities. Following his rescue from Le Chiffre, Bond convalesces at a glamorous private hospital. He is using a wheelchair and is dressed in pyjamas with a blanket over his lap: a significant departure from his usual image, indicating more marginal forms of masculinity. Where feminist-psychoanalytic theorist Barbara Creed (1993) identified images of *femininity* that trouble patriarchy – and Neale's analysis might lead us to see the injured man as "feminised" – Bond instead points towards Kaja Silverman's *Male Subjectivity at the Margins*, which considers "deviant" *masculine* bodies that disrupt hegemonic visual culture.

Silverman offers a more overtly Lacanian response to the "male gaze". Where Mulvey highlighted how patriarchy equates only femininity with "lack", Silverman importantly asserts that, because

Figure 3.3 Casino Royale – Spectacular masculinities

everyone undergoes symbolic castration (i.e., entry into the social order), lack is the condition of the psychoanalytic subject *as such*: what language gives with one hand it takes with another. This means that lack has "a range of possible representatives" (1992: 38), including forms of masculinity that offer "perverse" alternatives, "eschew[ing] Oedipal normalization" without regressing into narcissistic fantasy (2). In particular, Silverman highlights both the wounded and the enjoying male bodies as they refuse the dominant order: for example, narratives of the returning WW2 veteran bearing a "physical or psychic wound which marks him as somehow deficient, and which renders him incapable of functioning smoothly in civilian life" dramatise a kind of vulnerability not classically associated with the male hero (53); while the "masochistic ecstasy" of bodies that forgo mastery in the films of Rainer Werner Fassbinder offers another marginal kind of manhood (267).

Building on Silverman, we could recognise this range of "deviant" masculinities embodied in another war story: Hal Ashby's Oscar-winning Vietnam drama, *Coming Home* (1978), in which neglected military wife Sally finds emotional and physical connection with wounded veteran Luke. A spinal injury has left Luke paraplegic, but they nonetheless find a way to consummate their relationship in a pivotal and tender sex scene. While still deploying the conventional cinematic porno-grammar of close-ups on body parts, the scene presents a reconfiguration of intimacy based in both sight and touch, and with it a radically different model of masculinity as desiring and vulnerable at the same time. The image here stands in for what Luke is no longer able to feel: as he tells Sally "I want to see you", he is constituted as a different sort of "sexual protagonist" from the one identified by Berger. The camera lingers on the large scar on his back as he performs cunnilingus, offering a still too-rare mainstream cinematic image of a disabled man as sexual being. The flesh of Luke's "deficient" body thus challenges conventional masculine sexuality through its presence in the scene.

The Oppositional Gaze

While Mulvey crucially introduced the question of sexual difference to psychoanalytic film theory, and subsequent critics like

Neale and Brey expanded on this framework in relation to alternative identities and embodiments, the paradigm of the "male gaze" and its legacies did not satisfactorily attend to other forms of difference. As bell hooks notes in "The Oppositional Gaze", "Mainstream feminist film criticism in no way acknowledges black female spectatorship" (1992: 123). hooks echoes here both the directness of Mulvey's own intervention and the sentiment of Diawara's assessment of identification theory in the preceding chapter. hooks identifies the problem of what has come to be described as "white feminism", or a universalising tendency characterised by inattention to the impact of racial inequality when addressing gender imbalance. hooks presents "The Oppositional Gaze" as a corrective to this perspective, taking up an explicitly Foucauldian framework of "discourse" and "power" to address racialised difference in cinema. As we will see in the next chapter, such an approach would be understood as *anti-psychoanalytic* in its orientation; yet much of what hooks proposes can be read from a psychoanalytic perspective and seen as an invitation to expand the purview of psychoanalytic film thinking in relation to the insights of critical race theory.

In one respect, hooks does not challenge the fundamental claim of misogyny in film that Mulvey identifies as the "male gaze" but rather shows how it operates specifically in relation to black audiences. hooks notes that the scopophilic organisation of Hollywood cinema in fact allows black men to engage in those same voyeuristic structures: offering opportunities to look at white women without the threat of the lynch mob. hooks further notes instances of "black male independent filmmakers [who] represented black women in their films as objects of the male gaze" (118), and hooks' critique of Spike Lee in these terms is a longstanding feature of her work.

Against such reproduction of the *sexual imbalance* across what W.E.B. Du Bois called "the color line" ([1903] 2015), hooks posits the "oppositional gaze" as a critical attitude taken up by a spectator based in awareness of racialised as well as sex difference. hooks notes a similar ambivalence to Mulvey: recognising "enjoyment" in certain representations of blackness that were ultimately "degrading and dehumanizing", while also insisting on "contestation and confrontation" when faced with this white imaginary (1992: 117). For hooks, the "oppositional gaze" is a reclamation of the capacity of vision by communities that have historically been commanded *not to look*: taking ownership of one's own sight, once denied by slavery and colonisation.[6]

Such a *black look* offers both a mode of critical interrogation of white representations of blackness and the possibilities of an independent black cinematic alternative. For hooks and for Diawara, black viewers would experience a *rupture*: an antagonistic relation to white supremacist representations (and hooks explicitly compares this to the disaffection Mulvey experienced in the face of onscreen misogyny), which allows for critical distance from this racist imaginary and thus avoids the kind of collapse into masochism that Doane had identified in theorising masquerade. hooks points to Julie Dash's films, such as *Illusions* (1982) and *Daughters of the Dust* (1991), as creating space for the construction of radical black female subjectivity that we might also find with Kasi Lemmons, Cheryl Dunye, Mati Diop, or Michaela Coel.

Crucially, hooks suggests that such works "do not simply offer diverse representations, they imagine new transgressive possibilities for the formulation of identity" (130). This means transforming conventional film practices rather than simply inserting the proverbial "black faces in high places" of screen productions that otherwise maintain the status quo. For all of its many Afrofuturist charms, Ryan Coogler's *Black Panther* (2018), for example, does little in the end to disrupt what hooks calls the "white supremacist capitalist imperialist dominating 'gaze'" (129) in its promotion of patrilineage, oligarchy, and the CIA. By contrast, Barry Jenkins frames the no less mainstream production of *The Underground Railroad* (2021), funded and distributed by Amazon, and its attendant side-project *The Gaze* (an experimental film based on footage shot during the making of the series) as an explicit attempt to wrestle with the historical, social, political, cultural, and aesthetic legacies that "The Oppositional Gaze" identifies.

What hooks, Diawara, and Jenkins also suggest is the possibility of theorising a visual regime of the "white gaze" in homology with Mulvey. For example, Spike Lee famously observed that despite the diversity of the borough in which it is set Woody Allen's *Manhattan* (1979) is notable for its lack of black characters; while *Notting Hill* (1999) presents an elaborately staged sequence shot of a year-in-the-life of the West London district without any reference to the British Caribbean-led Notting Hill Carnival; and *Emily in Paris* (2020) initially offers a similarly whitewashed version of that city reminiscent of *Amélie* (2001) before it.

As we will explore through Žižek's theory of anti-Semitism in Chapter 5, the point of this critique is not simply to dismiss these portrayals as *inaccurate* (even while NYC, London, and Paris are of course far more diverse than such images suggest) but to ask what specific purpose such monochromatic representations might serve. The answer would seem to be the production of *white visual pleasure*: a cinematic imaginary constructed to support a spectatorial position that relies on blackness as a *non-position*; even while, as Richard Dyer suggests, *whiteness itself* is figured in Western visual culture as *empty*, "everything and nothing", an invisible yet omnipresent default (1997: 39). Bringing Mulvey and hooks together, then, we should recognise the sexless, effaced spectator of classical cinema as both white and male by default. And if Diawara suggests that "the dominant cinema situates black characters primarily for the pleasure of white spectators (male or female)" (1988: 71) – which is to say in the form of reductive stereotypes or as a contrast/support to the white protagonist's authority – then, where blackness is situated only as an *absence*, we can see such white visual pleasure as repeating at the level of representation the foundational logic of cinema itself as a technical apparatus (exposure of celluloid to light) gauged historically to the reflectivity of white skin and thus obscuring darker tones (Dyer, 1997: 82–144).

As we have seen, Mulvey's framework of the "male gaze" is often taken up as a theory of *spectatorship*, which is to say as a conceptualisation of the relation between cinema screen and a *notional* or *idealised* viewer: a subject position *posited by* the cinematic apparatus and the form/content of a film, rather than necessarily accounting for the experience of any given member of an historically-specific movie-going audience. How one responds, for example, to the masculinising or racialising pull of mainstream cinema depends on a variety of complex factors that critics and filmmakers such as hooks and Jenkins have attempted to address. Mulvey's framework is better understood as a theory of *aesthetics* rather than a theory of *spectatorship*. As an analysis of the formal organisation of classical Hollywood films as a *masculine cinematic imaginary* tending to construct, reaffirm, and reproduce the cultural gender norms of wider patriarchal society, "Visual Pleasure and Narrative Cinema" offers crucial insights. Women frequently are presented primarily as sex objects, and men as idealised vehicles for identification. In this respect, little has changed in the intervening decades: Mulvey's broader ideas are supported by mainstream, Western visual culture from the *Transformers* movies to the advertisements on every passing bus. What will be at stake for psychoanalytic film theory, however, is the metapsychological framework upon which Mulvey draws. Rather than belonging to *one who looks*, the "gaze", as we will see in the next chapter, is a property of *the visual field itself*.

Notes

1 For other important interventions on the sexual politics of spectatorship, see: Constance Penley (1989), Parveen Adams (1996), Elizabeth Cowie (1997).
2 I have avoided titling this chapter "Gaze" because it is a particularly contested term in psychoanalytic film thinking (see the next chapter, which could equally have been titled "Gaze" itself). I am tempted to suggest that a great deal of controversy might have been avoided if Mulvey had simply used a word *other* than "gaze" in describing the misogynist aesthetics of Hollywood – but her essay was meant as a polemic, and it has certainly served its purpose.
3 Barbara Creed famously proposed the "monstrous-feminine" as a Freudian development of the threatening/castrating aspect of the image of woman (1993); while Gaylyn Studlar took a Deleuzian approach to Freudian masochism to account for powerful feminine images that might otherwise be attributed to the voyeurism/fetishism of the "male gaze" (1993).
4 This conflation of "scopic drive" and voyeurism will be questioned in the next chapter.
5 See Tyrer (2025) for a detailed consideration of the film.
6 The next chapter will differentiate this use of "gaze" in its commonplace sense of *the act of looking* from the Lacanian concept of "gaze" as *object*.

Chapter 4

Object

Every art form, suggests Todd McGowan, "has a specific object. That is, it has an object that it treats as impossible within the field of experience that it depicts" (2020a: 229). This chapter will explore the cinematic object through Lacan's theorisation of the "*objet a*" in Seminar XI, *The Four Fundamental Concepts of Psycho-Analysis*. We will see how this framework depends upon two key details from Lacan's discussion. First: his recollection of time spent as a young man in a fishing town, where he took a trip on a trawler that led to a strange encounter with one of the crew. He relays:

> Petit-Jean pointed out to me something floating on the surface of the waves. It was a small can, a sardine can. [...] It glittered in the sun. And Petit-Jean said to me – You see that can? Do you see it? Well, it doesn't see you!
>
> ([1973] 1977: 95)

Second: Lacan's analysis of Hans Holbein's well-known painting *The Ambassadors* (1533): a *vanitas* composition traversed by a weird blot in the lower portion of the canvas, which is revealed to be a skull when viewed from the side.

In this chapter, we will see how Jacqueline Rose, Joan Copjec, Slavoj Žižek, and Todd McGowan have developed Lacan's ideas into an understanding of the cinematic object that entails a fundamental reconceptualisation of the "gaze": no longer as a mode of vision but as an object disturbing the visual field. This will

DOI: 10.4324/9781003399544-5

mean a conceptual shift: from conceiving of cinema as Lacanian Imaginary (associated with the "mirror stage") to an emphasis on what Lacan called the order of the Real. It is in this context, Žižek explains, that he "endeavours to demonstrate that the reading of Lacan operative in the 70s and 80s was a reductive one", while "there is 'another Lacan' [who] can contribute to the revitalisation of cinema theory (and of critical thought in general) today" (2001: 7). Such insights will allow us to draw a distinction between psychoanalytic film theory as it has been practised so far and the possibility of a new *psychoanalytic film thinking*, articulated around the question of enjoyment, and insisting that the gaze "is not an actually existing object; it is the distortion in the subject's visible field caused by the subject's perspective on that field" (McGowan, 2007a: 167).

Another Psychoanalytic Film Theory

This other strand of Lacanian thought in Film Studies can be traced back to the same intellectual milieu as *Screen* and Apparatus theory but running through different works and relying on distinctive concepts. Jacqueline Rose is an important figure here: a contemporary of Mulvey – publishing an article on adaptation alongside "Visual Pleasure and Narrative Cinema" – but philosophically more closely aligned with Copjec and Žižek. Rose's significance for psychoanalytic film theory is demonstrated by her 1986 book *Sexuality in the Field of Vision*, and in "The Imaginary" (first published 1981; original paper 1975) in particular, as both a critique of the framework founded on the mirror-stage and a preliminary sketching of a Lacanian alternative.

Reading Freud's paper "On Narcissism" and Lacan's "Mirror-Stage", Rose shows how desire intrudes on identification, both in theory and in practice, by introducing *lack* into this framework in relation to the object. Rose highlights the incompleteness of identification in the mirror-stage, noting that it requires an appeal: in "Remarks on Daniel Lagache", Lacan revisits the scene to show how the ideal-ego needs affirmation from the Other, indicated by the child's turn to their caregiver for recognition. The image is not in itself complete and is "defined in terms of this intrusion of the

Other" (Rose, 1986: 186), who is in turn *lacking* and cannot provide any final guarantee of one's being: the subject's desire is met only by a desiring Other. The mirror-stage does not *precede* desire but always exists within it.

Crucially, Rose cites Lacan's observation that the optical model of mirror reflections "throws no light on the position of the *objet a*" (quoted in Rose, 1986: 187), introducing a term that indicates a profoundly different frame of reference for psychoanalytic film theory. What Lacan calls *objet a* essentially corresponds to the Freudian "lost object" as what we imagine we give up as infants to enter the world of language: from a mythical state of plenitude and immediate relation to our object, to a social world in which we have the names for things rather than things themselves. The catch is, however, that we can only articulate this lack *through* language (i.e., I must use words to indicate what I cannot put into words), and our "object" comes into being only *through* this supposed loss. It only exists retroactively *as* lost and is thus *impossible* to recover. As Rose puts it, this signals "The precedence of the Real in the Lacanian scheme, as the point of the subject's confrontation with an endlessly retreating reality" (183). We find the Lacanian Real not in that *endlessly retreating reality* itself (as something that could potentially be returned to us) but in the *subject's confrontation* with this experience of lack: something that could *never* be restored because we never had it in the first place.

The key insight of Lacanian psychoanalysis is that once we obtain an object of desire, it loses its desirability and becomes dissatisfying: it can never fill the "hole in our soul" because this "hole" – the *lack* we feel as speaking beings – is what makes us who we are. We will continue to seek out other, better objects and yet they will always fail. As Rose notes, with this understanding "the notion of an imaginary plenitude [as in Apparatus theory] begins to be undermined" (182): instead, we face "the knots which the subject gets into in its attempts to elide or replace it – that Lacan terms the structure of desire" (183). We move from the "subject" as *ego* constituted in the mirror, to a subject of desire created through the repetition of lack. As a concept, *objet a* embodies this understanding: it is where the object of desire (*what* we want) meets the cause of desire (*why* we want) and is therefore sometimes referred to as the object-cause of desire. Yet it is not an *empirical* object (i.e., something we could hold in our hands); it is, rather, the name for the relation we have with objects. The *objet a* is something like what Freud's patient called the "shine on the nose" that excited him (SE 21: 152): a seemingly inexplicable X-factor (unconscious desire) that gives things their appeal.

In the last sections of her essay, Rose begins to consider what role such an object might play in film theory, as she moves away from Lacan's "Mirror-Stage" and towards Seminar XI as the defining point of reference. Rose mentions Lacan's encounter with the sardine can, and notes that his analysis of *The Ambassadors* shows how its composition "challenges the subject's fixed relation to the picture" (193): suggesting that these examples bring into question the idealised position of spectator. She turns this understanding on Metz's model of cinema, noting that Seminar XI undermines the idea of a spectator sitting safely at the point where images are presented to them for viewing (i.e., the model of Renaissance perspective); rather, the spectator is drawn into the visual field by the presence of something that cannot be grasped, a lack that would disturb any mirror relation. The "laws of perspective", Rose continues, tend to obscure both this "inaccessible object" and the subject's apparently transcendental position (that fullness described by Apparatus theory), but these laws also "contain a potential reversal" because desire pulls the spectator into the scene in relation to that very thing that cannot be seen, or what the image cannot show (the object-cause) (193).

This emphasis on desire challenges Metz's theory of cinematic perception because it changes the status of what is seen on the screen: where the imaginary signifier was defined in terms of absent objects made present by cinema, Rose's model "reveals the absence of the object" as such, as the *objet a* in the visual field (195). Even where Metz critiques the "delusion" of the "all perceiving subject", Rose suggests, he cannot escape the bounds of that idea, because he conceives of the spectator as "deluded by the nature of the perceptual phenomena, rather than by its very position as origin or centre of vision" (195). Rose concludes by noting "the ambivalent function which Lacan ascribes to the screen itself" as both site of "imaginary captation" and "sign of the barrier between the subject and the object of desire" (197). These ideas are sketched out only briefly in the essay, but they indicate the direction of a new psychoanalytic film thinking.

The Look and the Gaze

Lacan suggests that *objet a* can take many forms, principally corresponding to the objects of Freud's "partial drives" (e.g., oral/breast and anal/faeces). To these Lacan also adds "*la voix*" ("voice") as the object of an invocatory drive and the object of a scopic drive that he calls "*le regard*", usually translated as "gaze" ([1973] 1977: 242). Kaja Silverman considers this specificity of Lacan's thinking where she seeks to "differentiate the gaze from the look", to advance a paradigm that "differs in many respects from that which has dominated film theory over the past fifteen years" (1992: 125). While Mulvey had coined the term "male gaze" within a Lacanian framework, what she in fact describes is a relay of *looks* – from camera to actor to spectator – that assumes the same perspectival understanding of visual perception as Apparatus theory: the *optical model*, putting the spectator in an ideal viewing position where they seem to survey the world as a master of vision. Silverman observes that Seminar XI

> stresses not only the otherness of the gaze but its distinctness from what Lacan calls the "eye" or what I have been calling the "look" (the French language does not, of course, sustain my distinction, offering only one word – *le regard* – in place of the two primary English signifiers of vision: look and gaze).
>
> (129)[1]

Lacking an equivalent to "look" in French, Lacan refers to the optical model as the *eye* ("*l'œil*") to mark its difference from what he calls the *gaze*. While both English terms can be used to describe the act of seeing (I look, I gaze), the new psychoanalytic film thinking requires us to align *look* with the *subject* and *gaze* with the *object*. As Lacan states plainly: "*The* objet a *in the field of the visible is the gaze*" ([1973] 1977: 105).

The gaze reveals the inadequacy of the optical paradigm, standing – as Silverman notes – "as a monumental challenge to all such notions of mastery and immediacy" (1992: 146). Silverman suggests that Rainer Werner Fassbinder's films separate the look from the gaze, showing that *no one* possesses the gaze, no matter how central their look is to the scene. Fassbinder challenges the classical cinematic paradigm of the "male gaze" by depicting the desiring eye of women while equating masculine vision with lack of control. The gaze is situated outside voyeurism and always exceeds the look. Anticipating Iris Brey's more recent reflections, Silverman insists that feminism cannot simply demand a reversal of terms so that *men* are looked-at on screen, while adding the crucial Lacanian twist: "We have at times assumed that dominant cinema's scopic regime could be overturned by 'giving' woman the gaze, rather than by exposing the impossibility of anyone ever owning [it]" (152). The gaze does not belong to the eye, except as what it *cannot see*.

The Mirror as Screen

Towards the end of Silverman's chapter, however, discussion of the gaze turns to the work of Michel Foucault, which, she suggests, "enriches *Four Fundamental Concepts* immeasurably when it suggests that the field of vision may have been variously articulated at different historical moments" (1992: 152). For Joan Copjec, such a step would be wholly incompatible with the new psychoanalytic film thinking: an argument she sets out in her landmark essay "The Orthopsychic Subject: Film Theory and the Reception of Lacan" (1994: 15–38; first published 1989).[2] This work also addresses the problematic of the gaze but takes a different approach from Rose: first presenting a critique of Apparatus theory (and "Screen theory" as it incorporates Apparatus, Mulvey, Heath, etc.), and then beginning the elaboration of an alternative based once again in Seminar XI.

Copjec states that the "central misconception of film theory [is that,] believing itself to be following Lacan, it conceives the screen as mirror [but] operates in ignorance of […] Lacan's more radical insight whereby the mirror is conceived as screen" (1994: 15–6). To expose this misconception, Copjec revisits the concepts of *apparatus* and *gaze*. She begins by identifying what she calls the "Foucauldization" of Lacan by film theory (19): relaying a passage from *Re-vision: Essays in Feminist Film Criticism* (Doane et al., 1984), in which the editors reference Foucault's *Discipline and Punish* to observe that the situation of women under patriarchy is like that of the Panopticon, a prison designed by Jeremy Bentham to put each inmate in a cell that makes her permanently visible to a central watchtower. Although Copjec does not state this explicitly, we can see how this model is being conflated with Mulvey's "male gaze" and feminine to-be-looked-at-ness. Copjec notes that this "panoptic gaze" guarantees the total visibility of the subject within society, equating being *visible* with being *knowable*. Yet there is a flaw in this model because it relies on a circular logic (only what is visible is knowable and only what is knowable is visible) and, consequently, it excludes "invisibility and non-knowledge" from its worldview (1994: 17).

Copjec ventriloquises a counterargument: that the Panopticon *does* allow for the unknown because subjects are constructed by multiple "discourses" (e.g., education, law, medicine), the interactions of which cannot always be anticipated. The problem is that, in Foucault's framework, knowledge – and with it power – is produced *by* this very conflict between different discourses so there can be no possibility of resisting those institutions: "Differences do not threaten panoptic power; they feed it". The Lacanian position would be that social systems cannot produce something internally consistent/complete because they provide no external guarantee beyond their own symbolic structures. What is at stake is not the clash of external differences, the conflict between contrasting discourses, but "the fact that no position defines a resolute identity". Non-knowledge and invisibility are not found in the wavering between two different positions – which could be resolved by the production of new knowledge – but in (or as) "the undermining of every certainty, the incompleteness of every meaning and every position from within". This is what the Foucauldian panoptic model cannot account for: it is "*resistant to resistance*, unable to conceive of a discourse that would refuse rather than refuel power" (18). There is a fundamental incompatibility between Lacan and Foucault – who saw psychoanalysis as yet another way in which power apprehends the subject – and yet, Copjec claims, film theory has elided this difference in its conceptualisation of the "gaze".

Copjec then addresses *apparatus* as a turning point in Film Studies – a detailed argument which will be examined in the next chapter – before presenting an alternative framework that rejects understanding of the gaze as *visibility* in favour of the Lacanian gaze as *object*. She notes that in taking up the mirror stage essay film theory had overlooked Lacan's Seminar XI, which, in fact, offers a revised version of the mirror scene in the encounter with the sardine can. The "attack of anxiety" Lacan described in this anecdote indicates, for Copjec, that the gaze (represented by the floating object) "determines the I in the visible", although this should not be understood as making the I *fully* visible, as in the Panopticon, because "the subject *cannot* ever be totally trapped in the imaginary" (32).

Film theory cannot account for how the subject relates to what might be beyond the image. This turns out, in fact, to be *nothing*, but it is a consequential nothing. Lacanian psychoanalysis reveals the intersection of the optical model with the scopic drive as it produces "the subject's mistaken belief that there is something behind the space [of the image]" (33). While "Foucauldian" film theory conceives of the image as an inescapable prison house, "Lacan argues that the subject sees these walls as a *trompe l'oeil*, and is thus constructed by something beyond them" (34). Every act of looking implies a question: *What is it that I cannot see?* The scopic drive is the compulsion to see more; but there is *nothing* more to see, which only convinces us that *something* must be missing. This irreducible absence is "the point of the Lacanian gaze" (34). This is not an error that the subject can simply undo or overcome, because the subject is "the effect of the impossibility of seeing what is lacking in the representation" (35). I am caused by what I want to see, by my desire for what is not there.

This is how to interpret Copjec's characterisation of the *mirror as screen*: a screen is both something that *reveals* and something that *conceals*. It is a surface that makes things visible but also obscures what might be behind it. Copjec insists that this does not mean we are simply cut off from real objects by their representations – what Rose described as that *ever-retreating reality* – because "beyond the visual field, there is […] nothing at all. The veil of representation actually conceals nothing" (35). Film theory has located the "gaze" *in front* of the image, on the side of the spectator, who coincides with a point of full meaning and visibility; while, for Copjec, the gaze is "located 'behind' the image, as that which fails to appear in it and thus [...] makes all its meaning suspect" (36).

Copjec returns to the sardine can as a further critique of the Panopticon. She suggests that we are "cut off from the gaze" rather than coinciding or identifying with it. The gaze does not offer support or validation: "The horrible truth, revealed to Lacan by Petit-Jean, is that *the gaze does not see you*" (36). The Panopticon is not "filled with knowledge or recognition; it is clouded over and turned back on itself, absorbed in its own enjoyment" (36). This is certainly true, but Copjec omits a vital twist that Lacan adds to his story, which will help us to appreciate the full impact of the encounter with the gaze. Copjec makes a compelling case for rejecting film theory's "Foucauldian" model of spectatorship as representative of *either* psychoanalysis or cinema, but "The Orthopsychic Subject" does not elaborate the Lacanian alternative beyond an abstract level. To grasp what this other gaze – gaze as *objet a* – might look like in film, we must turn our attention elsewhere.

The Žižekian Blot

At almost the same time as Copjec, Slavoj Žižek published his own crucial intervention as "The Undergrowth of Enjoyment: How Popular Culture Can Serve as an Introduction to Lacan" (1989a).[3] Here Žižek addresses the legacy of psychoanalytic film theory associated with identification, fantasy, and suture (see next chapter), noting that the Anglophone reception of psychoanalysis had not yet dealt with the "break" in Lacan's thinking: shifting emphasis in the 1960s "from the dialectics of desire to the inertia of enjoyment (*jouissance*)", or from the interface of the Imaginary and Symbolic to the encounter with the Real as the "Thing [...] that resists all symbolization". Echoing Copjec, he suggests that Anglo-American film theory had relied on the early Lacan, while "French film theory over the last decade [i.e., the 1980s]" corresponds to the later Lacan in its "turn from the signifier to the object" (1989a: 7). He points to the work of Pascal Bonitzer and Michel Chion, as they explore gaze and voice as cinematic objects.

As we will see, Chion's analysis of film sound has subsequently received widespread attention in Anglophone Film Studies, while Bonitzer has remained largely over-looked (e.g., 1982). Žižek, for his part, includes Bonitzer's work in the collection, *Everything You Always Wanted to Know About Lacan (But Were Afraid to Ask Hitchcock)*, but in film theory and, indeed, the wider reception of Lacan since the 1980s, it has fallen to Žižek himself – as well as Copjec, Dolar, and Zupančič – to elaborate an understanding of the psychoanalytic object as *objet a*. This begins with Žižek's earliest work in English, titled simply "Hitchcock" (1986; first published in Slovenia, 1984). In it, we find in microcosm many of the ideas that Žižek would go on to explore in works such as *Looking Awry, Enjoy Your Symptom!*, and the *Everything...* collection. Crucially, Žižek introduces the notion of the "Hitchcockian blot" as indicating "the object-cause of desire, object small *a*" within the image (1986: 108): an innovation that will help us to develop a picture of what the "other" psychoanalytic film theory will be.

Cinema has therefore been central to Žižek's project from the beginning. His groundbreaking first book in English, *The Sublime Object of Ideology*, is developed through discussion of numerous films and was followed up by several works devoted entirely to the medium (1991a, 1992a, 1992b, 2000, 2001), culminating in his own screen adventures in collaboration with filmmaker Sophie Fiennes on *The Pervert's Guide to Cinema* and *The Pervert's Guide to Ideology* (2013). Nonetheless, a common complaint against Žižek is that he reduces films to *examples* of ideas and treats cinema no differently from literature or theatre: critics as diverse as Vicky Lebeau (2001), John Mullarkey (2009), and David Bordwell each insist that Žižek does not attend to the unique textual qualities of film. McGowan counters that cinema plays a vital role in Žižek's thought because it is where he practices his dialectical method, passing different ideas through those scenes from Hitchcock, Lynch, Tarkovsky, Kieslowski to find "the point at which the concept exceeds itself and reveals the contradiction that holds it together" (2014: 68). Yet even his staunchest defenders seem to concede the point regarding textual analysis and suggest that Žižek simply focuses on other questions, such as *enjoyment* (McGowan, 2007b) and *ideology* (Flisfeder, 2012).

But this would be to overlook the centrality of *form* for Žižek when he turns seriously to the question of cinema. At the Toronto International Film Festival in 2016, he explained his understanding of "cinematic thinking" in precise terms:

> film is thinking [...] where the form of a film has its own dynamic which does not simply, faithfully render [or] illustrate the narrative content but tells more: tells even what is excluded, censored in the content and so on. This tension between form and content is where cinematic thinking is located.
>
> (2016b)

This recalls Freud's emphasis on the role of the form in dreams: how desire makes itself present by distorting the substance of the dream through the dreamwork, rather than being found in either the manifest or latent content. As Žižek elsewhere elaborates,

> We only attain the level of proper dialectical analysis of a form when we conceive a certain formal procedure not as expressing a certain aspect of the (narrative) content, but as marking/signaling the part of content that is excluded from the explicit narrative line, so that [...] if we want to reconstruct "all" of the narrative content, we must reach beyond the explicit narrative content as such, and include some formal features which act as the stand-in for the "repressed" aspect of the content.
>
> (2019: 237)

Žižek develops this insight in relation to a range of filmmakers – from the contrast between the raw visual style and "kitsch" narrative of Lars von Trier's *Breaking the Waves* (1996) to the way that music enacts, rather than illustrates, the emotional excess of melodrama or the ending of Chaplin's *City Lights* (1931) – but his prime example of "thinking in cinema" is the interplay of subjective and objective shots in Hitchcock, from the murder of Detective Arbogast in *Psycho* (1960) to the God's-eye view of *The Birds* (1963), as it reveals the implication of the spectator within the spectacle. For Žižek, this approach shows that "I am formalist

[...] in the sense that, to understand the film, you should include into its content the message delivered by the autonomy of form. It's at that level that true thinking in cinema happens" (2016b).

This emphasis can be seen in the concept of the "blot" and the pivotal role it plays in Žižekian psychoanalytic film thinking. As first set out in "Hitchcock" and subsequently developed across his work, the blot – or the gaze as cinematic object – is revealed by the formal patterns of Hitchcock's work. Žižek suggests that the basic procedure of this cinema is to include something out of place within the image – such as the single windmill rotating the wrong way in *Foreign Correspondent* (1940) – that, when noticed, means "perfectly ordinary events acquire an air of strangeness" (1991a: 88). This leads Žižek to a theory of cinematic styles according to Freud's psychosexual stages.[4] First, classical realism as the oral stage: giving us an appearance of the natural rendering of reality that we "devour [...] with our eyes" (89). Second, montage enters at the anal stage: now we are shown fragments without the illusion of continuity, creating new meanings not dependent on the individual parts (e.g., the visual metaphors of Sergei Eisenstein's "intellectual montage"), and giving us something "to fill out the nothing, that is, to make up for what we do not have" (95). Hitchcockian suspense entails "passage to the 'phallic' stage" in the way that it introduces something that "sticks out" from the scene (89). Nothing objectively changes once we spot it, but normality is redoubled onto itself thanks to this incongruous detail: a surplus that renders the whole field suspect. Žižek compares this to the distorted skull at the bottom of *The Ambassadors*, as an "element that, when viewed straightforwardly, remains a meaningless stain" but when viewed from a particular angle reveals its meaning for the scene (90). In Holbein's case the dignitaries' riches are undercut by the *memento mori* of the skull; and in Hitchcock's, the sleepy Dutch countryside becomes the lair of an assassin due to the uncanny windmill turning against the wind.

Žižek suggests that the *tracking shot* – or the movement of the camera through space – is the "standard Hitchcockian *formal* procedure for isolating the stain" (93), identifying four variations of this process that separates a strange body from the surrounding reality. First there is "the usual tracking shot that endows the object-blot with a particular weight by slowing down the 'normal' speed and by deferring the approach", passing from an overall view of the scene to the particular detail, as in the steady movement towards the key in Ingrid Bergman's hand from *Notorious* (1946). This contrasts with the "precipitous" approach to the object, as in the two sudden jump cuts bringing us face-to-face with the eyeless corpse in *The Birds* (96). Žižek calls these the "obsessional" and "hysterical" modes of capturing the object *indirectly*: in each case, "we miss the object because of the speed, because this object is already empty in itself, hollow – it cannot be evoked other than 'too slowly' or 'too swiftly', because in its 'proper time' it is nothing" (94). Then there is the "reverse tracking shot, which begins at the uncanny detail and pulls back to the overall view of reality" (96), suggesting a world determined by an object that has now become obscure: e.g., the craning movement away from Teresa Wright in the public library of *Shadow of a Doubt* (1943) as the scene is filled with dread by a stolen ring. Finally, there is "the paradox of the 'immobile tracking shot', in which the camera does not move: the shift from reality to the real is accomplished by the intrusion into the frame of a heterogeneous object" (96), such as the gulls entering from "behind" the frame in that God's-eye view of *The Birds*. The birds themselves become the blot, turning the seemingly objective shot into a *bird's-eye view* that undermines the possibility of a safe or neutral perspective.

For Žižek, these formal techniques are equivalent to the movement of the spectator from the conventional viewing position *in front* of *The Ambassadors* to that disturbing, *oblique view* across the canvas that transforms the main image into a meaningless blur while revealing the truth of the composition in the skull. This distortion or "anamorphosis" of the skull is essential to Žižek's understanding of the "blot", which is revealed in a passage from Shakespeare's *Richard II*: "Like perspectives, which rightly gaz'd upon / Show nothing but confusion; ey'd awry / Distinguish form" (quoted in Žižek, 1991a: 10). The blot cannot be apprehended straightaway (the skull as distorted "confusion") but – as Bushy tells the Queen here – can only be perceived in its clear and distinct form by looking at it *awry*, by taking an indirect approach. The tracking shot is Hitchcock's cinematic method of *looking awry* at the blot, of revealing its anamorphic form within the picture, to make the gaze as *objet a* perceptible within the visual field.[5]

The gaze can only be

> perceived in a distorted way, because outside this distortion, "in itself", it does not exist, since it is nothing but the embodiment, the materialization of this very distortion, of this surplus of confusion and perturbation introduced by desire into so-called "objective reality".
>
> (12)

The gaze is the consequential nothing that marks the distorting presence of the subject within the world: in fact, it is "nothing but the way that the subject's desire deforms what it sees" (McGowan, 2016: 78). We are not normally aware of how our desire shapes what we perceive: this distortion must be *excluded* from our vision for it to gain coherence. Žižek cites Lacan as noting: "The field of reality rests upon the extraction of the object a, which nevertheless frames it" (1991a: 94). To return to Žižek's formalism, this missing element of the content enframes the picture itself. The gaze typically marks this blind spot within our vision that lends it the appearance of neutrality – being blind to our desire, we simply tend to assume that everyone sees as we see – while itself being "'objectively' nothing". It is only when "viewed from a certain perspective", such as from the side of the canvas or through the lingering tracking shot, that "it assumes the shape of 'something'" and thus becomes perceptible (12). McGowan suggests that it is the unique power of visual media – and, as Hitchcock shows, cinema in particular – to make the gaze visible within the picture in a way otherwise impossible in everyday life. The gaze is not strictly an "object" as such but the "shine" that certain objects take on in the visual field: the camera makes this fascinating shine *visible* thus indicating our desire.

I am in the Picture

The path of Hitchcock's tracking shot in revealing the blot is, for Žižek, "reminiscent of the structure of the Moebius strip" (1991a: 95): a twisting loop with only one surface, meaning that if we attempt to travel along it to reach the "other side" we eventually find ourselves back where we started, like Fred Madison at the beginning (and end) of *Lost Highway*. From the scene to the blot, we move away from reality towards the Real that nonetheless provides reality with its frame. It is an inversion demonstrating "the dialectic of view and gaze: in what I see [...] there is always a point where 'I see nothing', a point which 'makes no sense', i.e., which functions as the picture's stain"; the *twist* is that "here I encounter myself, my own objective correlative – here I am, so to speak, inscribed in the picture" (1992b: 15).

This is why McGowan (2014: 73) in fact finds the crucial example of the gaze elsewhere in Žižek's work, in a brief reference to *Psycho* from "In His Bold Gaze My Ruin Is Writ Large". In this lengthy discussion of "Hitchcock's Universe", Žižek picks out not Arbogast's murder, the shower scene, or even Norman peeping through the spyhole, but the aftermath of Marion's death as the moment in which we are forced to confront the Real of our desire (i.e., its disturbing truth is revealed to us):

> recall the well-known scene [...] where Norman Bates nervously observes the car containing Marion's body submerging in the swamp behind his mother's house: when the car stops sinking for a moment, the anxiety that automatically arises in the viewer – a token of his/her solidarity with Norman – suddenly reminds him or her that his/her desire is identical to Norman's: that his impartiality was always-already false.
>
> (1992a: 223)

Here the spectator is forced to abandon that illusion of a neutral viewing position assumed by Apparatus/Screen theory: "its purity [is] blemished by a pathological stain" (223), provoked by the hesitation in the car's descent and felt in the sudden need for it to continue. The disruptive presence – what had been identified as the "blot" of the tracking shot – now manifests not as a distortion of the image itself but in the interruption and dilation of time as we experience Norman's panic. As McGowan elaborates:

[Hitchcock] highlights the spectator's desire and aligns that desire with Norman's cover-up of a murder. He cuts to Norman's anxious face and thereby encourages the spectator to share Norman's desire for the car to sink. [...] Hitchcock [thereby] deprives the spectator of the illusion of psychic distance from what transpires within the diegetic reality.

(2015: 69)

This *alignment* of spectator and spectacle constitutes a moment of what was explored in Chapter 2 as *identification*, but the implications here are quite different: rather than identifying while remaining *absent*, as in Metz's strange mirror, the spectator is suddenly made to feel *present* within the image as they become aware of their desire.

It is this example that allows us to tie together the repeated references to *The Ambassadors*, Lacan's anecdote about the fishing trip, and the concept of the gaze as *objet a*, in a psychoanalytic theory of film that revisits and transforms previous thinking. Copjec took us up to the point in Seminar XI where Lacan recalled Petit-Jean's taunt on the fishing trip, "You see that can? Do you see it? Well, it doesn't see you!". But what was missing from "The Orthopsychic Subject" was Lacan's subsequent reflection: "To begin with, if what Petit-Jean said to me, namely, that the can did not see me, had any meaning, it was because in a sense, it was looking at me, all the same" ([1973] 1977: 95). We can understand how the glint of the sardine can suddenly made Lacan feel his own presence with the scene – as a young bourgeois intellectual among the fishermen – but this final reversal turns the story into a parable for his theory of the gaze. The optical model of sight is subverted by the psychoanalytic understanding of the role that desire plays in our vision. As Lacan summarises: "The picture is in my eye [...] But I am in the picture" ([1973] 1977: 96; translation modified). The gaze makes the viewer *present* rather than absent, disrupting the fantasy that we are somehow detached from what we see. We encounter the gaze when – like Lacan on the trawler, out of place in the scene but within the scene nonetheless – we become aware of our implication in this field, particularly when faced with some sort of disturbance within our vision. As McGowan puts it: "It is in the distortion of the picture that the subject is included, because the subject's perspective is responsible for distorting what the subject sees. No one can look without the distortion that desire causes" (2015: 74).

It is for this reason that Lacan turns to *The Ambassadors* as a "trap for the gaze" ([1973] 1977: 89), which the composition reveals to the viewer as they feel their own presence in the visual field. McGowan notes that the skull is "the point at which the spectator loses their distance from the painting and becomes involved in what they see, because the very form of the figure changes on the basis of the spectator's position" (2007a: 7). We must shift our view. Abandoning the fixed position of Renaissance perspective – and with it the paradigm of Screen theory – we see the skull only by moving *towards* the painting and looking *across* the canvas. Holbein's anamorphosis is exposed, but more importantly, as McGowan explains:

> the gaze reveals that Holbein did not just paint the picture for a neutral or impartial look. One must move to a particular perspective to see it, revealing that the position of the spectator counts within the painting. The painting itself takes the spectator's desire into account, and the skull is the point at which the spectator is involved in what she or he sees.
>
> (2015: 73)

The spectator must include themselves in the painting, then, only to find that they are in fact *already there.*

This is demonstrated by Žižek when he is put into the frame by Sophie Fiennes in the *Pervert's Guide* documentaries. The basic formal procedure of these works is to recreate a scene from the film under discussion – a boat crossing Bodega Bay for *The Birds* (Fig. 4.1), a hotel toilet for *The Conversation*, the freezing waters of the Atlantic for *Titanic* – with Žižek replacing the principal actor. His physical presence within the image allows him to embody the blot itself while explaining the Lacanian theory of *objet a*: putting psychoanalytic film thinking into practice on the screen.

Figure 4.1 The Pervert's Guide to Cinema – Žižek in the picture

It is for this reason that the *Psycho* example is so important: it compels the spectator to feel themselves being drawn into the screen through their desire as it coincides with Norman's. It also leads us to a re-evaluation of *Rear Window* in its conventional interpretation. Žižek identifies the moment that the object of fascination, the murderer Thorwald, *looks back* across the courtyard as opening the possibility of an encounter with the gaze *within the filmworld* because "Jeff loses his position as neutral, distant observer and is caught up in the affair" (1991a: 91). Again extending the idea of distortion beyond Holbein's optical effect, Žižek identifies Thorwald's "protracted movement" as he enters the apartment and advances on Jeff as a "rhythm of events [that has] undergone a kind of anamorphic distortion" (91): another dilation of time, like *Psycho*'s sinking car, that suggests the spectator's (i.e., *Jeff's*) implication in the scene. As Žižek elaborates elsewhere, Jeff's strange gesture of firing flashbulbs to deter the murderer should really be understood as a defence, through *excessive* visibility, against "making oneself seen". But when Thorwald tips him out of the window, "Jeffries in a radical sense falls into his own picture, into the field of his own visibility" as he plummets into the courtyard. This inversion means that he "changes into a stain in his own picture, he makes himself seen in it, that is, within the space defined as his own field of vision" (1994: 69). In this sense, Jeff really *is* a surrogate for the cinematic spectator but not in the way envisaged by Screen theory. *Rear Window* in fact reverses the Panopticon: it is the "all-pervasive eye who is terrorised" as the spectacle reaches out to touch him (1991a: 92).

The Real Gaze

McGowan builds on the advances of Copjec and Žižek, making the case for a decisive shift away from film theory based in the Lacanian Imaginary, and towards a psychoanalytic film thinking of the Real by offering a systematic approach to the relation between cinema and *objet a*. Filmmakers, McGowan notes, "make films not for their own pleasure but in order to appeal to the spectator's desire" (2015: 9). The attraction of cinema, then, is not in pleasure but *enjoyment* (what Lacan calls *"jouissance"*). In fact, enjoyment is antithetical to pleasure; it is what we get when pleasure fails or overwhelms us. It is the point at which we suffer our satisfactions or, indeed, find satisfaction in our suffering. This is the ultimate insight of Lacanian psychoanalysis as it is understood by Copjec, Žižek, and McGowan. If we are motivated by the object-cause of desire, then to actually *obtain* that object must be impossible because it is constitutively lost to us. And yet, we obtain many *objects of desire* over the course of our lives; we certainly derive pleasure from them, but this will fade and become disappointing because they do not, in the end, give us the satisfaction we were looking for. More than this, however, we *must* find them lacking because to obtain that final satisfaction – of having our desires truly realised – would be a disaster. We would lose all reason for being and fall into despair. We need to keep on desiring because this is preferable to having our dreams come true (which would be a *nightmare*). For this reason, we derive *unconscious enjoyment* from the failures of the object. While disappointment might be experienced *consciously* as unpleasant, even painful, the unconscious derives enormous satisfaction from this suffering. This is what allows us to keep on desiring, to keep looking for the object, and to be ready for disappointment once again. Far from being "pleasure-seeking animals", we are in fact *self-sabotaging subjects*: constantly searching for enjoyment even at the expense of our own wellbeing.

We do not, therefore, enter the cinema in search of pleasure – even while this may be our conscious motivation – but at the risk of enjoyment. This is indicated to us by the role of the cinematic object. Film appeals to our desire by promising us a glimpse of the gaze: if there were no possibility of an encounter with images that challenge or disrupt us, then cinema would have no allure. Equally, if a film offers a persistently traumatic experience, then the effect would soon become deadening: as is the hazard of "extreme" cinema (e.g., Gaspar Noé, Philippe Grandrieux), where transgression becomes the norm. Instead, cinema tends to play hide-and-seek with the gaze to entice the spectator. In showing us and telling us *something*, rather than *everything*, a film provokes us to look and listen, and to want to go on looking and listening as it unfolds.

In mainstream cinema, this is best exemplified by point-of-view cutting and the famous Spielberg Face: a character shown contemplating some incredible spectacle – e.g., Ellie Sattler before a once-extinct Brachiosaurus – as the camera dwells on their stunned reaction, cueing us to respond in the same way once the object of their look is subsequently revealed in a cut to the next shot. There *is* pleasure in the reveal, but the important moment is the one *preceding* it, where desire is stimulated by withholding something to provoke a want-to-see (gaze as object-cause). The boundaries of the frame institute a barrier within the visual field that the spectator yearns to overcome.[6] The Spielberg technique is about set-up and pay-off: realising desire through the delivery of the next shot. This does not reveal the gaze, however, but obscures it behind some empirical thing that instead becomes the object of vision. As McGowan notes, "This action of relying on the gaze and then hiding it is the chief ideological operation of cinema" (2015: 81).

Yet this structure also points to an alternative, where the gaze *is* made present and compels us to face *enjoyment*. Copjec argues that the gaze does not grant the spectator mastery over the visual field, as had been supposed by Screen theory. Such a model is appealing because it imagines an active subject possessing the passive object (as in Mulvey's model of sexual difference), but this is undone by an understanding of the gaze as marking the *failure* of mastery, where we are beholden to the object. McGowan suggests that the *active look* of film theory "obfuscates a much more disturbing alternative: the object drawing the subject toward a traumatic enjoyment—the enjoyment of total submission to an unattainable object" (2007a: 10). To learn where our enjoyment lies is traumatic because it goes against our self-understanding, but this is the powerful experience that cinema offers. McGowan develops this idea in the pointedly titled *The Real Gaze*, which identifies different kinds of encounter with the cinematic object – depending on the style, genre, and politics of a film – that fall into four categories: *desire, fantasy, integration*, and *intersection*.

The cinema of desire is articulated around *absence*, concerning what we do not see. The typical narrative arouses desire by producing gaps in knowledge, as in the detective story. But when he suggests that "To experience the cinema of desire is to experience what one doesn't have" (71), McGowan means something rather different. The erotics of cinema here – i.e., the way in which it produces desire – come from how the cinema of desire situates the gaze as something that we do not (and ultimately cannot) see. McGowan suggests that "in addition to concealing something [such as a murderer's identity ...] a narrative also conceals nothing, an emptiness that no empirical object can fill" (74). This irreducible element is typically found in the ambiguity and uncertainty of European art cinema, in films offering no straightforward closure or easy satisfaction. The cinema of desire "allows us to experience lack and absence as fundamental" (77), as in the elusive cinema of Alain Resnais, Marguerite Duras, or Michelangelo Antonioni.

In centring absence, the cinema of desire insists upon the necessary role of the *objet a* as *obstacle*, which is nowhere clearer than in Wong Kar Wai's *In the Mood for Love* (2000). Every love story, perhaps even *every story*, requires an obstacle: the barrier preventing the couple from coming together is what gives *impetus* (cause) for the narrative and is typically overcome at its climax. *In the Mood for Love* is significant as a love story that asserts *the primacy of the obstacle itself* by refusing to bring the couple together. The frame is constantly blocked or barred, divided by walls and doorways, visualising the emotional barriers between Chow and Su and putting the obstacle within the image itself (Fig. 4.2). The soundtrack works in the same way: the musical motif "Yumeji's Theme" repeats nine times throughout the film, but each time – except during the end credits – it is cut short before resolving: each time, it leaves us wanting more. The point of *In the Mood for Love* is not to *overcome* this yearning: the yearning *is* the point. In the end, we realise that the obstacle is not external but *internal*: the obstacle is always psychically preferable to the object because not getting what we want allows us to sustain desire. We enjoy the gaze in its frustrating absence because our jouissance comes from the deferral itself – the *quizas, quizas, quizas* of Nat King Cole's song on the soundtrack – rather than any kind of consumption.

This contrasts with the cinema of fantasy, which is articulated around plenitude. Fantasy "relieves the subject from the burden of lack", stabilising desire by staging for us a relation to the object that is not impossible but "simply out of reach" (81, 24). Yet the cinema of fantasy is not just the *inverse* of the cinema of desire, offering that easy closure which is denied by art cinema. Instead,

Figure 4.2 *In the Mood for Love* – Loving the obstacle

the cinema of fantasy is characterised by *showing too much*: it exposes the gaze as *excess*, revealing the unconscious fantasies that underlie and distort our social relations. In Michael Mann's films, McGowan finds an ethical potential in recognising that this excess cannot be eliminated, but he also shows in the extravagance of Federico Fellini how such an experience ultimately becomes stifling. The cinema of fantasy tends to offer a *surplus* that is either pacifying or disturbing (or both). For McGowan, Stanley Kubrick is particularly effective at revealing the hidden enjoyment of fantasy by airing our "dirty secrets" in public (19). In *Dr Strangelove* (1964) and *Full Metal Jacket* (1987), for instance, we see the fantasmatic underside of symbolic authority as the films show how such figures "get off" on the exercise of power. Despite this revelatory capacity, however, such a gesture "tend[s] to leave the spectator unscathed" because it does not cause them to recognise their own lack of neutrality (25).

Spike Lee demonstrates that such hidden libidinal investments extend to *all* subjects in *Do the Right Thing* (1989), where racist fantasies are shown to stain every social relation. For McGowan, this puts us into contact with the enjoyment of the Other, or the satisfaction to which we assume others have access but which eludes us. Fantasy gives us *another reason* why we cannot obtain the ultimate object: its staging erects a barrier between the subject and their satisfaction that *could* be overcome or, simply in its existence, gives a satisfying reason *why* the object cannot be obtained right now. It is no longer impossible but out there, somewhere. At the heart of racism is the fantasy of the enjoying Other: some exotic figure who has access to a form of satisfaction that we do not, either due to their secret knowledge and practices or because they are stealing enjoyment from us (McGowan, 2022).[7] Racist ideology, as we will see in the next chapter, is typically structured around the elimination of this Other who serves as a fantasmatic barrier to my own satisfaction. As Sheldon George (2016) argues, this allows the racist to extract enjoyment from the victimised Other: consciously the racialised figure is experienced as a terrifying threat, while unconsciously they offer an immense source of satisfaction. *Do the Right Thing* exposes this dynamic in its striking, direct address montage of characters hurling racist invective at the camera: the black guy complains about the Italians, the white cop about the Latinos, the Korean shopkeeper about the Jews, etc. In this way, we get an insight into the secret enjoyment of each group as it is fantasised by another.

The latter two categories in McGowan's typology involve different modes of relation *between* desire and fantasy in cinema, articulating our relation to the traumatic enjoyment of the gaze in radically divergent ways. The cinema of integration offers a fantasmatic solution to the impasses of desire. *The Wizard of Oz* (1939) is paradigmatic here: with Kansas as the dissatisfactory, monochrome world of desire, Oz the Technicolor fantasy of fulfilment, and the film's conclusion – where the characters of Oz coincide with those of Kansas – the point where a traumatic encounter with enjoyment is averted as desire is intermixed with the fantasmatic element (2007a: 156–7). The film serves to hide the gaze, as Dorothy is compelled to reconcile herself with everyday existence ("There's no place like home"). Hollywood is of course the key source of such libidinally pacifying cinema: where, for example, death and psychosis are impossibly overcome in Ron Howard's *Cocoon* (1985) and *A Beautiful Mind* (2001), and in Steven Spielberg's films a once-compromised father figure regains his symbolic authority, with Chief Brody in *Jaws* serving as the archetype. McGowan also finds such effects at the formal level in D.W. Griffith's cross-cutting technique: the infamous charge of the KKK in *The Birth of a Nation* – edited to show white characters making a "last stand" against actors in blackface, while the "knights" of the Klan ride to their rescue – is not only racist in content but also reactionary in form, relying on the movement between parallel scenes to create suspense and thus allow for the possibility of fantasmatic conclusion. The cinema of integration makes the gaze available only by transforming it into an ordinary object to be obtained (as in the Hollywood "happy ending"), thereby protecting us from its traumatic dimension.

Elsewhere, McGowan observes that in Mulvey's discussion of the "male gaze" we can in fact recognise the operation of classical Hollywood cinema as it serves to *obscure* the object: "the patriarchy manifests itself in the obfuscation of the gaze rather than in the manifestation of it" (McGowan, 2021). This recasts "Visual

Pleasure and Narrative Cinema" in a radical light: the "gaze" is no longer on the side of a purported male spectator but embodied by the woman on-screen. She is constructed to arouse desire, but this is really a defence against her troubling presence or what Mulvey called *castration anxiety*: a term Lacan rethinks in Seminar X, *Anxiety*, as indicating not concern over the prospect of *losing an object* but the uncanny emergence of the *objet a* in over-close proximity to us ([2004] 2014: 53).[8] Woman is no more the spectacle of lack than any other subject, but she is punished by the sadistic-voyeuristic look of the patriarchy for her very presence. The cinema of integration provides relief from the trauma of the object by containing or destroying it, moving us from an insecure to a protected world, thereby investing the subject in the maintenance of the status quo.

McGowan's interest lies mainly with the cinema of intersection, devoting not only a portion of *The Real Gaze* but also the entirety of its companion volume, *The Impossible David Lynch* (2007c), to the subject. This mode maintains a separation between the realms of fantasy and desire, "in order to reveal what occurs when they collide" (2007a: 163). What we find is the traumatic encounter with the gaze – not as absent or contained but directly appearing within the frame – and if the cinema of fantasy showed how enjoyment shapes our engagement with the world but ultimately left the spectator untouched, in the cinema of intersection we cannot emerge unscathed. McGowan suggests that, as with the *Wizard of Oz*, separation typically occurs at the level of form: different worlds or milieux suggested by different film stock, colour schemes, editing patterns, etc. but, unlike *Oz*, this distinction is maintained throughout so that when an element from one world appears in the other it is experienced as a disturbing intrusion rather than a pacifying amalgamation. *Blue Velvet* is again instructive here: the shadowy, threatening urban spaces of downtown Lumberton constitute the inconsistent world of desire, and the seemingly idyllic suburbia the abundant world of fantasy. The "intersection" occurs when Dorothy suddenly intrudes into Jeffrey's home life. Her naked and beaten body is a traumatic disruption of both the visual field and the Oedipal family/romantic structure: she seems to appear out of nowhere and exists within the frame as an impossible element, in whose presence the petty squabbles of Mike, Jeffrey, and Sandy seem insignificant. McGowan suggests that the film's strict separation of the two worlds makes Dorothy's unexpected presence even more disturbing. Intersection does not turn an impossible object into a possible one (as in integration) but simply allows the impossible to *happen*. In this way, it offers an encounter with the Lacanian Real as unbearable enjoyment (*jouissance*).

The cinema of intersection indicates the radical potential of cinema as an art form: it is the arena where we encounter the gaze proper and are reminded of our implication in the scene, as we saw with Holbein and *Psycho*. Interestingly, this often entails a form of *identification* with a challenging figure, as with Norman's anxious view on the sinking car. Other examples of the encounter with the gaze, for McGowan (2023), include the ending of *The Silence of the Lambs* (1991) – where our appreciation of Hannibal Lecter's pun, "I'm having an old friend for dinner" indicates our endorsement of his desire to *eat* the odious Dr Chiltern – and our alignment with the child murderer Hans Beckert at the end of Fritz Lang's *M* (1931), where he is isolated in the frame in contrast to a reverse-shot of the baying mob, revealing the incompatibility of the claims of the individual with the demands of justice (2015: 83–4). Here it would seem to be the *moral* rather than visual field that is distorted: we feel our implication in the scene, but it is not necessarily made manifest through a blot or disturbance of the image. But what is really at stake for McGowan is not so much cinematic identification with the problematic character (as discussed in Chapter 2), as it is the possibility for a psychic identification with the *objet a* itself as the source of our enjoyment: in approximation of the psychoanalytic cure.

The Object-Voice

The cinematic object is not limited to the gaze, however. Rose observed that the object-voice should also be of interest to film theorists (1986: 182), and, as Žižek highlighted, the work of Chion ([1982] 1999) has served as an important inspiration. Representing Screen theory here would be Silverman's *The Acoustic Mirror*

(1988), which considers the female voice in film. This study does for the soundtrack of classical cinema what "Visual Pleasure and Narrative Cinema" did for its image-track: drawing on psychoanalysis to highlight fundamental misogyny in representations of femininity in Hollywood. Men may be heard and not seen, placed beyond the images in the realm of voiceover, as in *The Magnificent Ambersons* (1942); while women must be both seen *and* heard, reduced to bodily presence like Lina Lamont, bound to her Bronx accent and ridiculed for it in *Singin' in the Rain* (1952). Silverman offers a critique of Chion's account of the maternal voice, uncovering (as Mulvey had done to Apparatus theory) the gendered assumptions in his understanding of embodiment/disembodiment, but *The Acoustic Mirror* (again like Mulvey) largely leaves unexamined the question of *objet a* in the perceptual field: now *aural* rather than visual.

Chion finds renewed importance with the neo-Lacanian thinking of film sound. In *A Voice and Nothing More*, Dolar turns to Chion's analysis of the "acousmatic voice" to examine the relation between subject and object. The term "acousmatic" means a sound whose source we cannot see – such as a radio playing in another room – but, Dolar notes, cinema demonstrates the uncanny nature of this experience. While the ideal of film production is usually to bond sound and image together seamlessly (i.e., synchronisation), "the very endeavour", Dolar insists, reveals that "they do not fit". The acousmatic voice "is not simply the voice whose source is outside the field of vision" – as in voiceover commentary or narration – instead, it is the voice insofar as it cannot be tied to the body (2006: 65). Dolar points to Chion's discussion of the mother's voice in *Psycho* as the "mother of all acousmatic voices" in its disturbing, free-floating presence. However, where Chion points to the moment of "disacousmatization" – where a voice is finally pinned down to a source, such as the threatening whistle finally meeting the whistler and thereby identifying the murderer in Lang's *M* – Dolar suggests that a sound cannot be attributed to a body quite so easily (67). Lacanian psychoanalysis insists that a voice is always in excess of the subject. When the speaking mouth is shown, all that is revealed is a void: as made apparent in those encounters where a person's voice does not match their persona. The sound does not belong to the subject, even while we associate one's subjectivity with one's voice. Cinema offers multiple experiences of the traumatic disarticulation of voice from body: from the men behind the curtains in *The Wizard of Oz* and *The Testament of Doctor Mabuse* (1933), to the nightmarish soundscapes of *Twin Peaks* (1990–1991), where Leland Palmer is reduced to bestial, desynchronised roars whenever BOB takes over; the voice-as-weapon in *Dune* (1984), and Club Silencio's song without a singer in *Mulholland Drive* (2000). In these moments, the voice as an object "appears in the void from which it is supposed to stem but which it does not fit" (70).[9]

Beyond *The Real Gaze*, McGowan extends his theory of the cinematic object to the Lacanian voice. Where the gaze can be understood as what is unseen in the field of sight, the voice as *objet a* is what is *unheard* in the field of sound (2015: 75). This is the voice as *obstacle*, made apparent by its absence as in the famous ending of *Lost in Translation*. As their ambiguous but intense relationship comes to a close, Bob whispers something inaudible into Charlotte's ear; she smiles and replies "OK", but we never learn what passes between them. As with the Spielberg Face, desire is stimulated by withholding (voice as object-cause), but *Lost in Translation* is far closer to Wong Kar Wai's cinema of desire in its final refusal of a payoff. McGowan suggests that the point is not that Bob communicates *and* cannot be heard but that Bob communicates *what* cannot be heard: the nothing of a shared lack that binds them together (2007d: 62). McGowan finds the further operation of the object-voice in *The Conversation* (1974), which allows us to discern how desire shapes *aural* perception as much as visual perception. Surveillance expert Harry Caul assumes that his recording of an adulterous couple claiming "He'd kill us if he had the chance" means that their lives are in danger; but when the woman's husband is found dead, Harry realises that what he'd heard was "He'd kill *us* if he had the chance" (justification for pre-emptive murder) rather than "He'd *kill* us" (fear of discovery). Harry hears the *objet a* in how his desire determined what he perceived: "The encounter with the voice strips away the neutrality of the aural field" (2015: 78). Finally, if we recall his idea that each artistic medium has its own object that it treats as impossible within its field of representation, then – for McGowan – the voice is the object proper to *silent cinema* in particular (see 2020c).

The Real of Sexual Difference

More broadly, a major contribution of neo-Lacanian thinking is the reconsideration of sexual difference, particularly through Copjec's "Sex and the Euthanasia of Reason" (1994: 201–36), Žižek's "The Real of Sexual Difference" (2002: 57–75), and Zupančič's *What Is Sex?* (2017). Here the vital point of reference is Lacan's twentieth seminar, *Encore* ([1975] 1998), which sets out the *logical* – rather than biological – categories of "sexuation": masculinity and femininity not as complementary categories of being but as mutually exclusive attitudes towards lack, or ways of occupying symbolic space in response to the antagonism of the Real. Rather than a model of conflict between genders based in power relations (as per Mulvey), neo-Lacanian thinking conceives of the logic of sexual difference as, for example, enjoyment based in eliminating contradiction or embracing it, social structures based on exclusion or openness, difference as a binary clash of external oppositions, or as the dynamic of each thing's alienation from itself (dualism or dialectics). The impact of this paradigm can be discerned in vital works of film theory such as Hilary Neroni's *The Violent Woman* (2005), Jennifer Friedlander's *Feminine Look* (2008), Fabio Vighi's *Sexual Difference in European Cinema* (2009), Frances Restuccia's *The Blue Box* (2012), and in my own work on feminine logic in cinema from dance to dialectical materialism (Tyrer, 2014; 2016: 91–139; 2019; 2023).

In the previous chapter, we considered Sciamma's work as "queering the 'gaze'", or a reworking of film aesthetics – that had historically settled into hetero-patriarchal patterns described by Mulvey – into new visions informed by, and more adequate to, the circuits of queer desire. This is certainly what *Portrait of a Lady on Fire* achieves, but the understanding of neo-Lacanian theory also brings a different perspective here, compelling us to recognise the *gaze itself* as queer. Freud's theory of the drive denaturalised sex by divorcing the aim of the drive from its object – i.e., its satisfaction does not depend upon a specific partner (SE 14: 122–3); while Lacan insists that procreation is a mere by-product of the detours of enjoyment ([1975] 1998: 120). Desire is not determined by gender, meaning – as Tim Dean observes – that psychoanalysis "poses a fundamental challenge to heteronormativity" (2003: 245). In his firebrand polemic *No Future*, Lee Edelman draws out this queer dimension in the Žižekian blot, characterising the heterogeneous onscreen appearance of Hitchcock's birds as an irruption of negativity into Bodega Bay. The obvious falseness of the matte compositing effect that puts the birds into the frame allows them to visualise that little piece of the Real where the gaze becomes the stain of enjoyment. For Edelman, jouissance has the queer force of negation, as it unsettles the socio-symbolic space: indicated here by the birds' violent attacks on children, as the latter represent the future-oriented ideology of compulsory heterosexuality and "reproductive futurism". The birds align with other, negating/child-averse figures such as Silas Marner, Ebenezer Scrooge, and Leonard from *North By Northwest*, who embody queerness in its capacity to figure "what [society] can neither fully articulate nor fully acknowledge" (2004: 26). This is also pursued by James Lawrence Slattery's *Taking Back Desire* (2025), which combines the insights of Copjec, McGowan, and Edelman to consider works such as *Sharp Objects* (2018) and *120 BPM* (2017): finding queerness in alignments between the socially abject and the aesthetically disjunctive that threaten to destabilise the logic of neoliberalism.

The new psychoanalytic film thinking reminds us that cinema is a medium of desire and enjoyment. Andrea Arnold's *Red Road* should be seen as a cinematic staging of the emergence of this radical film theory. Like the protagonist, Jackie, we began in the position of the all-seeing eye: as a CCTV camera operator, she spends her days in the guard tower of the modern Panopticon, observing those around her at a voyeuristic distance. Nonetheless, she finds that certain things are not visible to her eye – even with the power of the camera, there are areas of the field of vision that escape her sight and thus her knowledge – compelling her to look and look again. This leads to a traumatic encounter, as she spies

Clyde, a man she thought was still in prison for killing her husband and daughter in a car crash (Fig. 4.3). In glimpsing this impossible object, she finds herself drawn into the world that she observes: first stalking Clyde and attempting to exact revenge but then confronting him about their shared past and learning something of his lack in relation to hers.

In the same way, film theory must abandon understanding of the "gaze" as the act of looking and instead explore the uncanny presence of an object that disturbs our sight. Such an encounter with the gaze "means that spectators never look at the picture from a safe distance; they are in the picture in the form of this stain, implicated in the text itself". Rather than being viewable at arm's length, the image "sees you – takes into account your presence as a spectator" (McGowan, 2007a: 7). This complicates Laura U. Marks' conceptualisation of haptic visuality in contrast to an optical visuality that she associates with psychoanalysis, because it undoes the proximity/distance opposition that sustains her theory. Where she claims that "the Lacanian psychoanalytic model [...] castigates the 'overclose' viewer for being stuck in an illusion" (2000: 188) she is aiming at Screen theory. A properly Lacanian understanding of the gaze insists that we cannot "stand back", that we are – after all – always in the picture. For McGowan, how a film deals with the object –

Figure 4.3 Red Road – Impossible encounter

making it present, absent, obtainable, or traumatic – reveals its fundamental politics, and in the final chapter of this book we will address this question in detail as we turn to the topic of *ideology*.

Notes

1 Elizabeth Cowie: "The gaze is not the look, for to look is merely to see whereas the gaze is to be posed by oneself in a field of vision" (1997: 288).
2 McGowan reports that Copjec's work was initially presented at a 1988 conference attended by Metz and by Bellour, who was so perturbed by her paper that he felt unable to respond to it as had been originally planned (McGowan, 2015: 65–6).
3 This essay eventually became *Looking Awry*, in which Žižek acknowledges Copjec's influence, support, and encouragement (1991a: xi). Copjec and Žižek thus stand as the twin pillars of a new Lacanian film thinking inaugurated by Rose.
4 The experiences of infancy organised around the body's erogenous zones, as discussed in "Three Essays on Sexuality" (Freud, SE 7).
5 Žižek also proposes a "Hitchcockian Cut", which discloses the gaze through editing rather than camera movement (1991a: 117). Where the smooth continuity of the tracking shot produces radical discontinuity by introducing the disruptive presence of the blot *within* the frame, "Hitchcockian montage" makes it present *between* the frames. The cut is the formal inverse of the track but can also bring about an encounter with the gaze.
6 This is what is revealed by the Lacanian parable of Zeuxis and Parrhasios ([1973] 1977: 111–2): the curtain is a *trompe l'oeil* effect that tricks Zeuxis into believing there is something – his competitor's painting – that he desires to see beyond it. Parrhasios' painting thus manifests the gaze: an obstacle within the visual field provoking desire but ultimately concealing *nothing*.
7 Along these lines, we should redefine the "white gaze" identified in the previous chapter in terms of the distorting effect of the racist fantasy, through which – as Kevin Wynter observes – a bag of Skittles and hoodie turn a boy into a phantom threat (2022: 52).
8 McGowan re-reads *Vertigo* to show that when Scottie sees Judy put on Carlotta's necklace it becomes his own encounter with the gaze, as he realises that the spectacle of "Madeleine" had been created solely to appeal to his desire, while the shocked look on his face functions as gaze for the *spectator*, who has the possibility of an Other who might be shielded from the gaze taken away (2020b).
9 Žižek also pursues this idea in *Looking Awry* (1991a: 125–8), *Enjoy Your Symptom!* (1992b: 116–20), and elsewhere.

Chapter 5

Ideology

While Freud mentions "ideology" only in passing, he was nonetheless deeply interested in questions of social bonds and group beliefs,[1] and it was a central concern for many prominent thinkers that followed him, such as Wilhelm Reich, Herbert Marcuse, and Erich Fromm. Lacan has been equally influential on a generation of political philosophers from Louis Althusser and Alain Badiou, to Yannis Stavrakakis, Ernesto Laclau, and Chantal Mouffe. More recently, it has once again been the psychoanalytic interventions of Joan Copjec, Slavoj Žižek, Alenka Zupančič, and Mladen Dolar, as well as Todd McGowan and Mark Fisher, that have demonstrated the efficacy of critiquing ideology through popular culture – as in Žižek's memorable example of John Carpenter's *They Live* (1988), and via film itself in *The Pervert's Guide to Ideology* – and allowed for a wholesale re-evaluation of ideology, not as "false consciousness" divorced from reality but in terms of a reality that is itself fundamentally incomplete.

This final chapter will consider how cinema was seen by film theory to produce illusions of plenitude and mastery (i.e., to perform the function of ideology as such) and, crucially, by contemporary psychoanalytic theorists as a medium that could lay bare the points of failure within socio-symbolic reality itself. To present a chapter devoted specifically to ideology at the end of this book should not be taken to imply that it is somehow a separate concern from the discussion of identification, gaze, and enjoyment in the preceding sections. As we have already seen, ideology is a question that cuts through every stage in the development of psychoanalytic film theory, from Apparatus to Žižek, and from conceiving of cinema as technology of mass delusion to cinema as site for radical emancipation. This understanding begins by recognising that to practise psychoanalysis in Film Studies is never neutral.

Return to Lacan

The resistance to psychoanalytic film theory was immediate. From the journal's publication of "The Imaginary Signifier" to their resignation in 1976, four editors of *Screen* repeatedly protested the journal's turn towards Freud, Marx, and the avant-garde. As we have seen, however, cine-psychoanalysis flourished through the 1970s and '80s, before reaching a further crisis point in the 1990s with the embrace of cognitivism in mainstream Film Studies and philosophy in speculative approaches to cinema. By 2004, Todd McGowan and Sheila Kunkle declared, "Within film studies, not only has Lacanian psychoanalytic theory disappeared, but theory as such has given way almost completely to historicism and empirical research. The discipline has become, as David Bordwell and Noël Carroll prophesied in 1996, post-theoretical" (2004: xii n1). This was reiterated by Richard Rushton, who noted that, "the engagement between psychoanalysis and cinema has, to a large degree, disappeared" (2002: 107), and Žižek, who read the decline of the status of psychoanalytic film theory as an "indication of the decline of cinema studies" (2001: 31).

Yet it is with precisely such theorists that the fate of psychoanalytic film theory now rests. In *The Fright of Real Tears*, Žižek launches a robust defence of psychoanalysis and the need for renewed engagement with film theory. Writing in 2001, he notes that "the principal contradiction of today's cinema studies" is between "Theory" and the reaction against it in Bordwell and Carroll's "Post-Theory", which explicitly defines itself in opposition to psychoanalysis (2001: 1). Nonetheless, Žižek suggests, the critique of Post-Theory should be understood as "The Strange Case of the Missing Lacanians" because the Lacanian "Theory" described by Bordwell and Carroll is unrecognisable (1). It is a straw man, an effigy of Mulvey and Silverman, who were themselves largely working with a narrower version of Lacan's early thinking. Žižek complains that, "as a Lacanian, I seem to be caught in an unexpected double-bind: I am, as it were, being deprived of what I never possessed, made responsible for something others generated as Lacanian film theory" (2).

Rather than succumbing to his doom, however, like Burt Lancaster in a grubby motel room in *The Killers* (1946), Žižek offers an alternative course of action: "what if one should finally give Lacan himself a chance?" (2). Just as Lacan insisted upon a *return to Freud* to oppose the rise of "ego psychology" – a derivation of psychoanalysis advocating for strengthening of the ego as the goal of analysis – Žižek calls for a *return to Lacan* to open a new field of theoretical and practical possibility. In both cases, the necessity of such a turn is not just a wish for scholarly accuracy – to replace misinterpretation with correct reading – but a political imperative. Ego psychology, as a corruption of Freud, functioned as the handmaiden of consumer capitalism, ensuring conformity of the patient to the demands of the social order by fostering an illusory sense of self, while Lacan's elaboration of psychoanalysis insisted upon the radicality of the unconscious and its opposition to commodifiable social utility. Žižek identifies in Post-Theory a similar complicity with the status quo: such "modest" claims for "academic professionalism" in screen studies constitute an outright rejection of "political engagement" (13) and indicate a naïve desire to return to a state of prelapsarian innocence – before Marx and before Freud – where issues like the symptom and overdetermination are evaded. Žižek says: "for the cognitivist post-theorists, the demise of theory is experienced as a relief from a nightmarish burden" (14). Post-Theory is both an admission of intellectual defeat in the face of complex ideas, and the sign of an apolitical conservatism that refuses to engage with the problems of the world in a meaningful way.

Žižek notes that Carroll describes his own approach as "dialectical": characterised as progression through dialogue and debate between competing "theories" (that *marketplace of ideas* in Chapter 2). "What separates dialectics proper", Žižek notes, "from its cognitivist version is the way the subject's position [is] inscribed into the process" (15). Post-Theory relies upon the illusion of a neutral field of observation, surveyed by a detached researcher dispassionately weighing up the data (i.e., *it excludes the subject*). By contrast, the dialectics of Žižek's Hegelian-informed Lacanian theory – what we explored in the previous chapter as the object-gaze – insists upon recognising the role that the subject plays in constituting (and thus distorting) the field of observation itself: even the problems of "middle-level research" are shaped by desire and framed within certain ideological contexts. As we have seen, this point distinguishes a radical psychoanalytic paradigm from historical psychoanalytic film theory and Post-Theory alike.

Bordwell subsequently responds to this critique in a lengthy polemic published on his personal website that aims to dismiss Žižek outright. John Mullarkey characterises this conflict as what Jean-Francois Lyotard called a *"differend"* (2009: 60), or a dispute between two parties speaking incompatible languages who can never come to common understanding: *a case of Bordwells are from Mars, Žižeks are from Venus.* Yet such a compromise cannot be sufficient. As Žižek notes, "the antagonism between Theory and Post-Theory is a particular case of the global battle for intellectual hegemony" between critical theory on the one hand and "cognitivists and populisers of hard science" on the other (2001: 2). Žižek suggests that the challenge posed by Theory to the narrow empiricism of Post-Theory aligns with a tradition of scandals from Socrates' "corruption" of Athenian society to what Freud identified as the three blows to human narcissism dealt by Copernicus, Darwin, and psychoanalysis itself.[2] And if a critic as once ardently anti-psychoanalytic as Steven Shaviro can return with "The Cinematic Body REDUX" (2008) to close ranks with his Theoretical comrades, uniting Deleuzians and Lacanians alike against the anti-intellectual onslaught of Post-Theory, then the stakes of the dispute become clear. The violent reactions against such "epistemological shocks" are attempts to neutralise their radicality and maintain business as usual. Žižek's critique is thus two-fold: Post-Theory misses the mark in terms of its own critique of psychoanalysis, and it is part of a wider trend seeking to separate politics from knowledge.

The Ideological Cinematic Apparatus

Ideology has in fact *always* been the subject of psychoanalytic film theory. We should recall that the full title of Jean-Louis Baudry's 1970 essay (discussed in previous chapters) is "Ideological Effects of the Basic Cinematographic Apparatus". Coming out of a French intellectual climate in the wake of the May 1968 riots and the turn by influential film journal *Cahiers du Cinéma* towards Marxist criticism, this work – in addition to introducing the ideas of the dream-cave and screen-mirror – also sets out a materialist analysis of cinema in opposition to the "idealist" understanding of film as *revealing* the world (i.e., Bazin's filmic "realism"). Baudry, as we saw, suggested that camera technology "assure[s] the setting up of the subject as the active center and origin of meaning" ([1970] 1974–1975: 40). In a version of the psychoanalytic-Marxist philosopher Louis Althusser's notion of "interpellation", the apparatus "hails" me: it calls me into being as a spectator through the effect of its construction.[3] Cinema produces a picture that appears to be composed for me, as I occupy a perfect position to see it: as "transcendental subject". As a result, I am blinded to the fragmentary nature and constructedness of the film. Optical technologies tend to conceal the ideological effects they produce: a finished film does not allow us to see the "work" that has been done to translate raw reality into cinematic product (i.e., we see the world as images recorded and projected, rather than the recording/projection process itself). Erasing labour and making what is artificial seem natural (as in the smooth flow of images in classical cinema) are key functions of ideology, understood – with Marx and Engels ([1932] 1976) – as the ruling ideas, serving to ensure that the conditions in which the existing state of things can be maintained and reproduced.

This leads Baudry to a common conclusion at this point in history: that revealing the mechanisms of production within the frame (e.g., by showing the recording camera) "would produce a knowledge effect" causing a "denunciation of ideology" ([1970] 1974–1975: 41). These strategies are aligned with " political modernism" (see Rodowick, 1988) – modelled after Bertolt Brecht's "alienation effect" and suggesting that being reminded that we are watching a film has a radical impact on the spectator, as it shatters the "illusion" of cinema – and correspond to a surge in self-reflexive political filmmaking in the 1970s, such as the "counter-cinema" of Jean-Luc Godard and Jean-Pierre Gorin's *Vent d'est* (1970) and *Tout va bien* (1972).[4] The important reasons why such approaches failed to have a transformational effect will be the subject of the rest of this chapter.

Against the Imaginary Relation

Copjec's "The Orthopsychic Subject" addresses this framework explicitly where she notes the shared understanding of *apparatus* between Althusser and film theory. Althusser suggested that ideology represents an "imaginary relation" between ourselves and society through which institutions encourage us to accept the world around us and our places within it *as they are*. For Apparatus theorists, the same basic principle holds: "The representations produced by the institution of cinema, the images presented on screen, are accepted by the subject as its own" (Copjec, 1994: 21). Spectatorship here seems to work with the double meaning of "property" as *an aspect of myself* and *something that belongs to me*, which "allows the subject to see in any representation not only a reflection of itself but a reflection of itself as master of all it surveys". As Copjec adds, "The imaginary relation produces a subject as master of the image" (21).

Copjec identifies the problems with this film theoretical paradigm. As we saw in previous chapters, *narcissism* plays a central role as the mode of the spectator's relationship to the screen – "the subject sees itself as *supplying* the image with sense" while "it seems also to be an image of the subject's perfection" (22, 23) – yet, if screen-identification is a vehicle for rapport with the social order, then narcissism – as the turn towards the self and source of conflict with others – is at odds with this process and might seem to frustrate ideological entrapment. More importantly, Copjec notes that Seminar XI challenges "the argument that the cinematic apparatus, in direct line with the camera obscura, by recreating the space and ideology of Renaissance perspective, produces a centred and transcendent subject" (32). While film theory, Althusser, and Lacan might all agree that the apparatus produces an *illusion* of a subject at the vantage point for which the picture is organised, they disagree on *how* the spectator occupies this position. For Althusserian film theory, "the subject is installed in its position of misrecognition [...] without hint of failure" (32); it wholly and unerringly takes up the invitation extended by cinema. For Lacan, however, the subject is *not* reducible to this seat – "I am not simply that punctiform being located at the geometral point from which the perspective is grasped" (quoted in Copjec, 1994: 32) – and so there is always something in excess of the spectatorial position. This, for Copjec, also highlights the difference in conceptions of desire between Lacan and *Foucault* (her essay's main target): with Foucault seeing desire as a function of the *success* of the social order in producing a subject, while Lacan situates desire at the point of the Law's *failure*. If the subject produced by the Panopticon were produced *completely* and unable to act otherwise, then their surveillance would be unnecessary.

At this point, film theory's Althusserian tendencies start to coincide with those Foucauldian aspects explored in the previous chapter – where the "male gaze" was compared to a Panopticon-like regime of total visibility for women on screen – but this is also where to draw some important distinctions. Apparatus theory similarly introduces an all-seeing eye, but as we saw in Chapter 2, it is the *spectator* that takes up the panoptic vision of the camera/projector rather than being subjected to it: cinema, in this understanding, effectively puts us in the *guard tower* to survey the visual field in its entirety. This point remains somewhat latent in "The Orthopsychic Subject", but it does seem related to the "ambiguity" that Copjec identified in how we understand the image as "belonging" to the spectator: in the mirror-screen relation, it is an image of me *and* an image for me. In my cinema seat, I would become *both* prisoner and guard of the Panopticon at the same time.

This leads to a further problem, indicating perhaps the most fundamental misunderstanding in the appropriation of psychoanalysis by film theory. In taking the mirror-stage as its model – and in making its dynamic a question of *visual mastery* – Apparatus/Screen theory enacted a subtle shift *away* from what Lacan describes and towards the panoptic model. Where identification with the mirror-image was supposed to give the child a new sense of mastery *over its own body* – the image of seeming completeness being taken up as preferable to the child's own experience of incoordination, which is why Lacan refers to a *bodily ego* – the apparatus is thought to give the spectator *mastery over the visual field* itself while the body fades away in the experience. We shift from an understanding of self-mastery *through* the image (Lacan) to mastery *over* the image in the cinema. It is this simple difference that opens the door to what Copjec calls the "Foucauldization" of film theory and the attribution to psychoanalysis of a position that it never held. In fact, as the new Lacanian film thinking makes clear, the insights of psychoanalysis constitute a challenge to mastery at every level.

The Politics of the Gaze

Copjec's argument also echoes that of Mladen Dolar's "Beyond Interpellation". Although not addressing film theory, Dolar takes aim at the theoretical underpinnings of the apparatus in Althusser's notion that *ideology interpellates individuals as subjects* (1971: 170). When the apparatus of the state works on us to internalise ideology and produce us as subjects *to* that system, Dolar suggests, the process "is never complete – the clean cut always produces a remainder" (1993: 77). Althusser's model does not account for this surplus: it sees the individual as wholly captured by ideology. For psychoanalysis, however, this remainder *is* the subject in both senses of the term: it is the topic proper to Lacanian theory and (or rather *because*) it is where we find the psychoanalytic "subject" as a psychological-embodied being. Dolar explains: "the subject is precisely the failure to become the subject – the psychoanalytic subject is the failure to become an Althusserian one. For Althusser, the subject is what makes ideology work; for psychoanalysis, the subject emerges where ideology fails" (77–8). This surplus that cannot be accounted for by interpellation is indicated by the *objet a* as both the "motor of any ideological edifice" and its "structural problem": ideology is the attempt to integrate this object to form a harmonious symbolic system, but this is impossible because the object persists as a fault in the structure (i.e., the failure of interpellation). This means that ideology "is situated in an irreducible gap which cannot be healed. Whatever comes to fill this gap has no natural or legitimate affinity to it; it is in this impossibility that ideology and its critique are situated" (92).

The way that a film deals with this object – in the form of the gaze – determines its politics, and, for McGowan, cinema "becomes ideological [in Marx and Engel's sense, above] when it obscures the gaze rather than when it highlights it" (2015: 75): i.e., the difference between *integration* and *intersection* explored in the previous chapter. Screen theory understood spectatorship in terms of a mastering look, giving us the impression of a coherent visual field existing independently of us and thus reaffirming the illusion of atomised individualism characteristic of capitalist ideology. On this latter point, McGowan would in fact agree: ideology does not simply misrepresent the world – as in "false consciousness" (see below) – but "functions by obscuring the subject's involvement in the world that it experiences. It presents the world as fully formed prior to and apart from the subject's desire" (75). The crucial difference between psychoanalytic paradigms here lies in the role of the gaze: Screen theory saw the "gaze" as the problem, aligning it with the apparatus and the mastering look, while psychoanalytic film thinking sees the object-gaze as the *solution*, offering a way to challenge ideological enclosure. If the apparatus forms a meaningful whole, then *objet a* is the meaningless hole within the whole. Understood as marking the distortion of the world caused by the subject's desire, the gaze reminds us that we are part of what we see: "Without the investment of subjects in it, the world would cease to function, and ideology must work to perpetuate this investment without revealing the dependence of the world on the subjects who constitute it" (75). An encounter with the gaze allows me to perceive that I am *of* the world and the problems within it; and if I am part of what I see, if I have a role in constituting it, then I also have a role in changing it by challenging the status quo. While popular cinema mostly "works to hide the gaze and limit cinema's disruptive potential" (75), the very fact that it *must* be hidden still attests to its radical potential.

This does not mean, however, that the most politically effective modes of filmmaking are those offering relentless encounters with the gaze or announcing its presence in an overt manner. For McGowan, "radical filmmaking works in the exact opposite way from the Brechtian *Verfremdungseffekt*. Instead of alienating spectators, the most important films lure spectators in to an encounter that they would otherwise consciously avoid" (2020a: 301). This takes us back to the *dream* because cinema, uniquely like the dream in this regard, leads us into situations beyond our conscious control where the unconscious might take over. Such lack of control could seem to "[render] the spectator extremely vulnerable to ideological manipulation while at the cinema" (2007a: 13). This would be the position of Screen theory. However, for McGowan, this is to misunderstand the relationship between consciousness and ideology: "One does not resist ideology through the act of becoming conscious; instead consciousness is itself a mode of inserting oneself into ideology and avoiding one's desire" (13). Screen theory – and with it, political modernism – emphasised an increase in consciousness, producing knowledge of our situation by telling us *this is only a film*. Yet, McGowan reminds us, Freud observed that "When the thought 'this is only a dream' occurs during a dream, ... it is aimed at reducing the importance of what has just been experienced" (quoted in McGowan, 2007a: 13). Similarly, "cinema that draws attention to its own artifice and shocks the spectator with constant self-awareness" (15) – such as Godard and Gorin's work – increases critical distance and produces knowledge but does not bring about a relinquishing of conscious control that might allow for a truly transformative encounter with the gaze; while cinema that constantly bombards the spectator with trauma will alienate them to such an extent that they simply leave the cinema.

Instead, McGowan suggests, we should *submit* to the film like a dream, opening ourselves up to those points where it might disturb us. It is only through full immersion that we can be brought to a place of rupture, indicating the presence of our enjoyment and attesting to our lack of mastery.[5] Such an encounter could even occur during a violently regressive film – for example, the presence of the obviously plastic baby undercutting the overtly propagandistic message of *American Sniper* – and may well *not* occur in explicitly Leftist cinema, as we have seen. But this encounter can come about wherever we experience the failure of ideology to fill in the gaps of our socio-symbolic reality: as in McGowan's example of *The Thirteenth Floor* (1999), where protagonist Douglas Hall discovers the crude wireframe model at the edges of his (now apparently *virtual*) world (2020d). As we will see with Žižek, such *constitutive incompleteness* is the space in which freedom becomes possible. Before this, however, we should turn to another attempt to account for the dynamic of lack and plenitude in the cinema as ideology machine.

Back to the Suture

The concept of "suture" was central to psychoanalytic film theory of the 1970s and '80s but is now virtually forgotten. *Screen*'s 1977 "Dossier on Suture" marked an unprecedented moment in Film Studies, putting pure psychoanalytic theory at the centre of a leading Anglophone venue for academic film analysis. The dossier included Jacques-Alain Miller's "Suture (Elements of the Logic of the Signifier)" in a first English translation – by Jacqueline Rose, no less – which remains the version of reference today. Not itself a work of film theory but a contribution to the philosophy of psychoanalysis written by Lacan's son-in-law, the article serves as a conceptual touchstone for the texts accompanying it: Jean-Pierre Oudart's "Cinema and Suture", an application of Miller's ideas to film predating even Baudry's work on apparatus, being first published in French in 1969; and Stephen Heath's survey of the field, "Notes on Suture".

Recasting Miller's analysis of the relation between the subject and symbolic structure as a version of the relation between spectator and screen, Oudart defines suture as "the closure of the cinematic énoncé" ([1969] 1977: 35). Put another way, suture is what allows us to understand the flow of images making up a film as a *meaningful whole* rather than just a succession of unrelated fragments. Oudart identifies three main modes of suture: the "subjective" cinema of classical Hollywood, using the continuity system to join sequences together; the disjunctive editing of

Godard, which simply undoes classical continuity; and Robert Bresson's cinematic articulation of shots, where slight mismatches between character point-of-view and camera position "[indicate] the spectator's own position" (45). More generally, Oudart identifies suture as a logical relation within the image: we encounter the shot as a field of pure plenitude, where anything might happen; but it is also haunted by what he calls the "Absent One" or the realm off-screen that we cannot see and makes us aware of the image's frame as a *boundary*. This is collapsed by the introduction of another shot giving further meaning to the first, perhaps revealing something of the absent field, or establishing a new one. In either case, the Absent One persists and in this way *lack* is inscribed into the system of images.

While Heath demonstrates a nuanced engagement with Oudart, and Kaja Silverman elsewhere explores the concept through an extended reading of Hitchcock (1983: 195–236), it is the version elaborated in Daniel Dayan's slightly earlier article, "The Tutor Code of Classical Cinema" (1974), that dominates conventional understanding of suture in film theory. It is here that the concept is framed explicitly in relation to *ideology* while being reduced to a simpler framework mapping neatly onto the opposition between Hollywood and avant-garde. Dayan focuses on the role of point-of-view in classical cinema, arguing that the shot/reverse-shot technique serves to stitch us into the filmic experience: with a first shot opening a space for the spectator that is then closed off by a complementary second shot. Once again cinema interpellates us as subjects of ideology by smoothing over the rupture of film form that we might experience in the *cut*, and thereby obscures the work, the constructedness of the film. Against this, Dayan cites *Vent d'est* as a film that refuses ideological suture by continually making us aware of its cinematic processes.

Yet, if we go *back to the suture*, as Žižek puts it, to examine the specifics of Miller's argument and then trace the concept's re-evaluation in *The Fright of Real Tears* and *Concept and Form*, then we can unpick it from historical psychoanalytic film theory and think it anew. Miller's essay develops Lacan's brief references, for example, in Seminar XI to "suture" as "a conjunction of the imaginary and the symbolic" ([1973] 1977: 118) to develop a theory of the symbolic order. Miller notes that all such systems must include an element standing for a surplus: that which does not fit into the system or where the system does not work. His example is "zero", which is different from all the other numbers yet, when counted ("there is *one* zero"), generates all the other numbers ("zero and one is *two*", etc.) ([1966] 1977: 30). In this way, lack is inscribed within the symbolic order, providing a stand-in for the subject within the system as the gap which is not *closed up* but *sutured into* the structure.

While some of this sense *is* retained by Oudart, Žižek notes that the term now functions as a vague synonym for "closure", signalling "that the gap, the opening of a structure was obliterated, enabling the structure to misperceive itself as a self-enclosed totality of representation" (2012b: 153). And where Screen theory saw cinematic suture as the "production of a subject" (Heath, 1977: 58) as in ideological interpellation, for Miller it is how the subject's presence is registered as a fault in the system. Žižek suggests that the operation addressed as suture in film theory should be understood differently in relation to the shot/reverse-shot – as situating a subjective point-of-view within the objective cinematic space to avoid the trauma of a free-floating perspective comparable to Chion's acousmatic voice (Žižek, 2001: 33) – while observing that Miller's theory could be compared to the Marxist understanding of "how the politico-ideological struggle is inscribed into the very heart of the economic process itself. It is precisely this that Marx called 'class struggle', and this is why he speaks of '*political* economy'" (Žižek, 2012b: 158). Suture would then register the point of *failure* within the ideological system, rather than its totalisation or enclosure.

Significantly, Žižek also makes an original contribution to film theory here with his concept of "interface", as the point where "the exchange of subjective and objective shots fails to produce the suturing effect" (2001: 39). His discussion begins with the uncanny effect of the giant photo of Charles Foster Kane looming over Kane himself at the election rally in *Citizen Kane* (1941), as if he "is redoubled by his spectral shadow"; before turning to Kieslowski as "the great master of making the spectator perceive this dimension of interface in an ordinary scene" (39). Rather than introducing some supernatural effect into the story, Kieslowski reveals the spectral dimension of everyday reality itself: from the larger-than-life reflections in the post office screens in *Decalogue 6* (1989) and the replication of the heroine's face in the train window in *The Double Life of Veronique* (1991) – "her perturbed state presaging her impending heart attack is signalled by the barely perceptible distortions of what we see through the train window due to the uneven glass surface" (50) – to *Three Colours: Blue* (1993) and the extreme close-up of Julie's eye as it fills the screen. Within her eye, we see the reflection of a doctor telling her that her husband and son have died. For Žižek, this presents interface as the "shot which contains its own counter-shot[.] It is no longer diegetic reality which contains its suture-spectre; it is reality *itself* which is reduced to a spectre appearing *within* the eye's frame" (52).

Interface, however, is not just the condensation of shot and reverse-shot within the frame; what is at stake is this *spectral* dimension introduced into the image,

> evoking the idea that there is no cosmos, that our universe is not in itself fully ontologically constituted, and that, in order to maintain an appearance of consistency, an interface-artificial moment must suture-stitch it (a kind of stage-prop that fills in the gap, like the painted background that closes off reality).
>
> (53)

Žižek compares this to the back of the painting visible in Velázquez's *Las Meninas* (1656) and to *The Silence of the Lambs*, where "Lecter is seen as a spectre reflected on the glass pane across from Clarice" (40). When such a shot occurs, there can be no reverse-shot and thus no "suture" in the traditional sense. For Žižek, the interface produces the *objet a* as reality's fantasmatic supplement within the frame – and it is this latter point that will prove crucial to our thinking of ideology.

The Trashcan of Ideology

We have started to see the limitations of theories of spectatorship and society depending on a certain kind of *knowledge* produced with *critical distance* to address a problem of mass delusion. What is required here is not only a new theory of cinema but also a new theory of ideology. This is where Žižek's film thinking becomes indispensable. In *The Pervert's Guide to Ideology* (*TPGI*), Žižek notes:

> According to our common sense, we think that ideology is something blurring, confusing our straight view. Ideology should be glasses, which distort our view, and the critique of ideology should be the opposite like you take off the glasses so that you can finally see the way things really are.

This would be the model of ideology as "false consciousness": the ruling values of the age simply give us the *wrong idea* about the world. People do not realise this and so go about their lives acting according to these mistaken beliefs, captured in Marx's famous line, "They do not know it, but they are doing it" (quoted in Žižek, 1989b: 39). Here, the aim of emancipatory politics would be to *educate* people about how the world really works, and then they would rise together and overthrow their masters. This is the vision of revolution offered by *The Matrix* (1999), where we can *wake up* from the ideological illusion and escape our servitude. However, major revolutions rarely happen, and in the general course of things we tend to *keep calm and carry on*: we largely *know* how the world works but little seems to change.[6]

To account for this – and to elaborate an alternative, more adequate theory of ideology – Žižek turns to John Carpenter's *They Live* as "one of the neglected masterpieces of the Hollywood Left" ([1997a] 2008: xi). The film shows homeless labourer John Nada as he discovers a box of strange sunglasses, which – as Žižek puts it – "function like critique of ideology glasses" (*TPGI*). Through the lenses, Nada's world is transformed into black and white, revealing propaganda messages all around him: dollar bills announce, "THIS IS YOUR GOD", while billboards declare "OBEY" and "MARRY AND REPRODUCE". As Žižek notes,

> To see the true nature of things, we need the glasses: it is not that we have to take off ideological glasses in order to see reality directly as it is – we are "naturally" in ideology, our natural sight is ideological.
>
> ([1997a] 2008: xiii)

Where the *Matrix* model of false consciousness seemed to suggest that we can find a space outside of ideology, that we can be free of it entirely and stand in what Morpheus calls "the desert of the real", *They Live* reveals that ideology is how we spontaneously experience reality itself. There is no outside: "In ideology 'all is not ideology (that is, ideological meaning)', but it is this very surplus which is the last support of ideology" (1989b: 124). The ultimate trap is to believe that we find freedom *beyond* the ideological frame. As Lacan suggests, *the non-duped err*: those who believe they are not "duped" are the ones who are in error. Whenever a person claims to be acting without ideology, we can be sure that they are most embedded within the ideological structure.

Reality is always accessed through the mediation of ideology, which has the function, in psychoanalytic terms, of *fantasy*: "for something real to be experienced as part of 'reality', it must fit the pre-ordained coordinates of our fantasy space" (1993: 43). In our present era, Mark Fisher (2009) characterises this fantasy space as "capitalist realism": the ideological reality constructed by neoliberal capitalism to ensure its own reproduction by making it appear that *there is no alternative*. This does not mean that there is no such thing as external reality, however. We must simply include fantasy as part of reality. In fact, we cannot do without fantasy because in its absence we would lose reality itself.

Yet ideology is not simply a veil of illusion cast over our world. Where Žižek identifies enjoyment as a "political factor" (1991b) this suggests that ideology, in its function as fantasy, structures our libidinal investment, our psychic "buy-in" to the social order. The socio-symbolic field gives the subject an *answer* to the enigma of their desire. It produces conformity by telling us what to do, where to go, what to buy, etc., thus relieving us of the burden of everyday existence and guaranteeing our identity as individuals. But ideology also offers avenues of enjoyment through what we saw Žižek, in Chapter 2, call the "built-in transgression, its unacknowledged obscene support" (2006: 85): those unwritten rules that can be safely ignored – in fact, must be violated – to signal one's membership of the group. Žižek points to the Hays Code of censorship, which ostensibly banned references to sex, drugs, and crime in Hollywood but nonetheless permitted numerous dirty jokes, implied scenes of adultery, etc. by "[codifying] their enciphered articulation" through visual metaphor and innuendo (84), as in the infamous "horse racing" exchange from *The Big Sleep* (1946). Ideology thus works as fantasy by fixing our symbolic coordinates and structuring our enjoyment.

We are unable to escape this condition and so we require a shift in perspective – like putting on dark glasses – to see how the ideological fantasy structures our reality. Žižek notes that "when one looks for too long at reality through critico-ideological glasses, one gets a bad headache: it is very painful to be deprived of the ideological surplus-enjoyment" ([1997a] 2008: xiii). In fact, we will struggle very hard to maintain this investment. When Nada tries to convince his friend, Armitage, to put on the glasses in a rubbish-strewn alleyway, he tells him: "I'll give you a choice: either put on these glasses or start eating that trashcan".[7] Armitage resists, in a ludicrously extended fight scene, suggesting to Žižek that he *knows* he is duped by the ideological fantasy but is unwilling to give up his enjoyment within it. Simply exposing the bare facts of the social situation is not sufficient: as Žižek explains, "In vain do we try to break out of the ideological dream by 'opening our eyes and trying to see reality as it is'". Instead, to "break the power of our ideological dream" is "to confront the Real of our desire which announces itself in this dream" (1989b: 48).

Capitalism and Enjoyment

We can see how the ideological fantasy structures reality – and how this depends on the "underside" of enjoyment – in Boots Riley's Afro-surrealist anti-capitalist masterpiece, *Sorry to Bother You* (2018). The protagonist, Cassius "Cash" Green, finds a job at RegalView: a grubby telemarketing company, employing salespeople on a commission-only basis to flog encyclopaedias and self-help manuals. RegalView is a typical capitalist enterprise. It operates by wage theft as Squeeze, the film's labour organiser character, recognises when he tells his colleagues: "We make the profits, and they don't share". And yet, it is not the *injustice* of this system that is its most salient point. As McGowan notes in *Capitalism and Desire* (2016), rather than focusing on what

Ideology 113

capitalism *denies* us, the key to understanding here is precisely in what it *does* offer instead.

This is suggested on Cash's first day at work. As he hesitantly enters the building, his attention is soon caught by something off-screen: he stops in his tracks, eyes widening – the object of his look then revealed in a reverse on a longer shot of a golden art deco-style lift, with a well-dressed man and woman standing beside it (Fig. 5.1). This is, of course, the classical cinematic grammar of *desire*, using point-of-view cutting to provoke a fascination also carried by the shimmering musical cue that highlights the moment. The entrance to *Cash's* workspace is down a flight of stairs to the basement, but something else – something much more preferable – is being signalled in this moment. This allure is explained, within moments of Cash sitting at his desk, by his manager's orientation spiel: *Do real good and you might make Power Caller.*

As McGowan observes, the "fundamental gesture of capitalism is the promise": the promise of future returns on investment, the promise of a higher salary and nicer house, the promise of untold pleasures unlocked by the next commodity (2016: 11). In each instance, "the future embodies a type of satisfaction foreclosed to the present and dependent on one's investment in the capitalist system" (12). Those gold doors and the glamour of the Power Caller are the first terms of the capitalist promise being extended to Cash: even before he has donned his headset, there is the

Figure 5.1 Sorry to Bother You – Promise of capitalist enjoyment

seductive possibility of something else, something better to come. Squeeze recognises this workplace messaging as a "scam", but it is also much more than that; it represents the fundamental libidinal economy of the capitalist system, the psychic offering that allows it to reproduce and endure.

Capitalism holds its subjects forever on the verge of realising their desire but never actually reaching the stage of full satisfaction: there is always a newer iPhone or a nicer car on the horizon. But, of course, we *enjoy* this dissatisfaction because, to recall the previous chapter, the pursuit of the object is always psychically preferable to its capture. However, this does not mean that capitalism is simply an expression of "human nature"; rather, the capitalist system exploits this self-defeating quirk of the psyche to keep its subjects in a state of constant desire with the promise of "a more complete satisfaction [...] just around the corner" (11). Capitalism proposes *accumulation* as the best means of reaching that satisfaction, inducing the psychic buy-in that is required to ensure the continuation of the status quo. Cash tells his customers that purchasing his everyday commodities will give them what they are looking for: the leather-bound encyclopaedias will get you laid, while the wellness series will cure your husband's cancer. As Power Caller, he makes the same pitch to his clients: you can make more profit if you just invest in the goods and services we offer. This is the perspective of the "regal view": a vantage point on ever-greater luxury just out of reach. RegalView couches its libidinal offer in the ideology of *success*: work your way up to Power Caller and you will be that much closer to the ultimate satisfaction. It is no accident that the managers point upwards – as to the heavens – when they describe this trajectory: they are invoking that sublime transcendence of old religion, now available through the corporate incentive structure rather than the Sunday service (225). In this way, Cash's employers are not just typical but *paradigmatic* of traditional capitalist logic.

The persistent question for emancipatory politics is of course: If we know that we are being exploited in this way, *why isn't every worker a revolutionary?* As we have already seen, this has frequently been treated as a problem of *knowledge*, but what is vital about *Sorry to Bother You* is how it emphasises the limitations of that approach. Later in the film, Cash uncovers evil billionaire Steve Lift's plan to bioengineer a species of half-human, half-horse "Equisapiens" to constitute the ideal working class for his logistics company, WorryFree. Cash spreads his message throughout the media but within 24 hours Lift is hailed a business genius and WorryFree stocks "skyrocket at a rate faster than any other company in history". Cash despairs that he put the problem "right in front of their faces [...] and nobody gives a fuck"; while, in a moment marking *Sorry to Bother You* at its most didactic, Squeeze observes that, "if you get shown a problem but have no idea how to control it, then you just decide to get used to the problem". This is a vital point but potentially remains within the paradigm of *knowledge* without addressing *enjoyment*, which, as McGowan notes, is precisely where capitalism's efficacy lies.

WorryFree's stock price rises because of the promise of satisfaction to which it is indexed: the Equisapiens will bring more efficient labour and better shareholder value. This is reiterated by Lift's own performance of satisfaction on the TV news: his Tom Cruise-like exuberance providing an embodied demonstration of the libidinal offering made possible by this "miracle" breakthrough. Nonetheless, as Marx suggested, the bourgeoisie produces its own gravediggers: Lift's affective display here offers us a way to deal with the problem. Looking at *Sorry to Bother You* through the psychoanalytic lens shows us that revolution cannot be *desired*, for this would be to install capitalism as the *obstacle* and necessary source of our unconscious satisfaction: a position frequently evinced in contemporary anti-capitalist discourse.[8] Instead, we must mobilise *enjoyment* in a radical way.

Sorry to Bother You concludes with Cash, now transformed into an Equisapien himself, leading the vanguard assault on Lift's mansion and sarcastically turning around the telemarketer's apology – "Sorry to bother you!" – as he kicks down the door. But we should pay attention to *how* Cash gets here: he unwittingly snorts the activator chemical at Lift's party, yet his transformation is not immediate. It is, in fact, only once he has divested himself from the capitalist libidinal economy that the revolutionary change can occur. At the film's dramatic climax, Cash helps to free the horse-people and unionise the workers of RegalView, perhaps suggesting a reformist "happy ending" where success through "incremental change" coincides with *getting the girl*, as once estranged partner Detroit now returns to his affections. But what is more important is the day *after*, where we see Cash embrace a more modest way of life: returning to his uncle's garage accommodation, wearing plainer clothes, and giving away his ill-gotten Maserati by way of apology for previous class treachery. He tells best friend Sal, "I've got a car that'll do me just fine", gesturing to a smaller Ford hatchback.

Cash refuses the capitalist fantasy of success and promise of full satisfaction to come, recognising instead his enjoyment in the object's inadequacy. As McGowan suggests, "For this type of subject, the fact that the car has a dent in the fender and hesitates going up hills becomes the source of the satisfaction that it provides" (2016: 40). *Sorry to Bother You* suggests that once accumulation is no longer paramount, once the psychic appeal of capitalism begins to fade, political action becomes more likely. We need not necessarily change into Equisapiens, but with the mobilisation of *enjoyment* change as such becomes possible.

Given its radical political message, *Sorry to Bother You* is notable for its combination of *both* counter-cinema *and* narrative cinema techniques. If we compare it to Peter Wollen's (1982: 79) "cardinal virtues" and "deadly sins" of cinema, we can see that, on the one hand, *Sorry to Bother You* largely observes linear storytelling and offers no major barriers to identification; while, on the other, it offers foregrounding in the reflexive use of over-dubbing to create its celebrated "white voice" effect, excessive multiplicity in its eclectic mixture of genre codes and stylistic conventions, and an important degree of aperture in its multi-stage ending. Significantly, *Sorry to Bother You* demonstrates the radical potential of *fiction*. Rather than *departing* from reality, it is properly *sur*-realist: a heightened form of experience as a means of interrogating the world. Riley's film is truly revolutionary in its approach to *form*: tempering enjoyment with pleasure to ensure that its spectator stays the course, engaging us in – rather than alienating us from – the contemporary political conversation.

The "Logic" of Anti-Semitism

If, as McGowan suggests, ideology's function is to give us a reason for the existence of lack (2020d), then under neoliberal capitalism – as in *Sorry to Bother You* – that "reason" is meritocracy (just work harder to succeed) supported by the promise of better enjoyment (accumulation). However, when this socio-symbolic structure breaks down – as we are seeing increasingly today as the "promise" of hard work no longer offers the payoff of a better tomorrow – ideology offers a *different* kind of reason for lack. To explain this, Žižek returns us to *Jaws*. He notes that the film's shark attacks have been interpreted in various ways: as a metaphor for the climate crisis, an intrusive foreign threat, or even the violence of capitalist exploitation. "So which is the right answer?", Žižek asks.

> I claim none of them and at the same time all of them. [...] The function of the shark is to unite all these fears so that we can in a way trade all these fears for one fear alone. In this way, our experience of reality gets much simpler.
>
> (*TPGI*)

This shows that we should pay less attention to the *content* of an ideological formation than to its *function*, which reveals here that the shark "is homologous with the anti-Semitic figure of the Jew: 'Jew' is the explanation offered by anti-Semitism for the multiple fears experienced by the 'common man' in an epoch of dissolving social links" (1993: 148). Rather than addressing the complex reasons for the crumbling of the symbolic edifice, which would entail the wholesale rethinking of a way of life, it is far easier to put the blame on a (usually marginalised) Other who is said to be blocking the proper functioning of society.

Žižek examines this dynamic in *The Sublime Object of Ideology*. Here he argues that the social fabric is, in fact, *always* "traversed by an antagonistic split which cannot be integrated into the symbolic order" (1989b: 126), because it is founded on the originary cleft of class antagonism and economic exploitation. What is at stake in the ideological fantasy is a vision of society as a cohesive whole: such as the "corporatist vision" of the social body, to which each class contributes according to its function. How, then, to account for the distance between this vision and the antagonistic struggles of society? The answer is to "displace social antagonism into antagonism between the sound social texture [...] and the Jew as the force corroding it" (125). They are the *thieves of jouissance* identified in the previous chapter: stealing or barring access to enjoyment. And so, according to this pernicious dogma, society can only be redeemed by destroying this object.

This impossibility of a cohesive society is given body by the anti-Semitic figure of the Jew, which is, Žižek suggests in *The Plague of Fantasies*, "*the* example of the sublime object" because it lays bare the fundamental structures of the ideological formation. He identifies this figure as the "object as a negative magnitude", a "mere positivization of a void". It is, he suggests, "the elementary procedure of the critique of ideology" to recognise this, and to understand that, of course,

> it is not the Jew who prevents Society from existing (from realizing itself as a full organic solidarity, etc.); rather, it is social antagonism which is primordial, and the figure of the Jew comes second as a fetish which materializes this hindrance.
> (1997b: 97)

The "Jew" is a *sublime object* of ideology, but, Žižek adds:

> We must remember that there is nothing intrinsically sublime in a sublime object according to Lacan, a sublime object is an ordinary, everyday object which, quite by chance, finds itself occupying the place of what he calls *das Ding*, the impossible-real object of desire. The sublime object is "an object elevated to the level of das Ding". It is its structural place – the fact that it occupies the sacred/forbidden place of jouissance – and not its intrinsic qualities that confers on it its sublimity.
> (1989b: 194)

The significance of this is two-fold. Firstly, the anti-Semitic figure of the Jew has *nothing to do with Jewish people* but refers to a particular structural position. It is not enough to combat anti-Semitism simply by stating, "*But Jews aren't like that!*". Once we engage in a debate at this level, the steel trap of racism has snapped its jaws shut around us: we have accepted its premise and are now bound to the terms of its discourse. If we attempt an anti-racist critique only at this level, we have already failed. We must recognise the purpose that "Jew" serves as an ideological figure covering up the inconsistency of the system. Secondly, any seeming confirmation of the anti-Semitic stereotype is entirely beside the point: we are not dealing with the details of lived experience but an unconscious fantasy formation. Žižek compares this to a case of pathological sexual jealousy: even if one's partner *really is* unfaithful, "this does not change one bit the fact that [such] jealousy is a [...] paranoid construction" (48). The paranoiac fantasy *precedes* and determines any experience of reality, rather than the other way around.[9]

Žižek suggests that the final stage of ideology critique is traversing the fantasy. This does not mean *going beyond* fantasy, passing through it entirely to reach a non-ideological other side. Instead, it means going *into* the fantasy as far as possible to identify the kernel of enjoyment at its heart. He states, "we must recognize in the properties attributed to 'Jew' the necessary product of our very social system; we must recognize in the 'excesses' attributed to 'Jews' the truth about ourselves" (1989b: 128). This entails recognising our own role, our own investments in the world, which will allow us to discern the contingency (rather than necessity) of the current social order. The very existence of ideology is in fact a testimony to our *freedom*. The function of ideology is to cover up its own failure by rationalising the irrational: it is "the enumeration of a network of reasons, masking the unbearable fact that the Law is grounded only in its own act of enunciation" (Žižek, 1997b: 100). In Lacanian terms, *there is no Other of the Other*, no external guarantee of our symbolic structure: nothing to verify its claims to authority and therefore nothing to fix our positions or identities within it. McGowan suggests that "Our ability to contest an ideological structure depends on our ability to recognize the real point at which it breaks down, the point at which the void that ideology conceals manifests itself" (2007a: 17). We have seen throughout this book how film places us in a unique position to apprehend this, or as Žižek puts it at the close of *The Pervert's Guide to Cinema*:

> In order to understand today's world, we need cinema, literally. It's only in cinema that we get that crucial dimension which we are not ready to confront in our reality. If you are looking for what is in reality more real than reality itself, look into the cinematic fiction.

Notes

1 Brief references occur only in *Civilisation and Its Discontents* (SE 21: 97) and *The New Introductory Lectures* (SE 22: 67). Freud does, however, theorise the binding force of identification with a leader in *Group Psychology* (SE 18: 105–10) and in *The Future of an Illusion* (SE 21: 5–56) characterises religious belief as libidinal investment in illusion not dissimilar to false consciousness.
2 The Earth is not the centre of the universe (Copernican heliocentrism); humans are not unique among the animals (Darwinian evolution); and "the ego is not master in its own house" (Freudian unconscious) (SE 17: 143).
3 Althusser's example in "Ideology and Ideological State Apparatuses" is a person on the street turning around when they hear a policeman calling out, "Hey, you there!". Whether or not they were the intended target of the hail, they are *interpellated* – called into being by the apparatus of the state – in this moment of turning around. Schools, churches, and the media also serve the same function, for Althusser, of producing us as subjects (1971: 174).
4 Peter Wollen (1982: 79–91) defines counter-cinema as fragmentary, open-ended, and self-referential, in opposition to the linear, closed, and unselfconscious or "invisible" style of Hollywood.
5 The point, however, is not simply to *go on dreaming* once we find the moment of rupture but to allow this moment – which could not have been accessed otherwise (i.e., through critical distance) – to mark an *awakening* for our thinking about cinema.
6 Žižek – following Peter Sloterdijk – suggests that this can lead to *cynicism*, where the subject is "quite aware of the distance between the ideological mask and the social reality, but he none the less still insists upon the mask", the formula of ideology then being: "they know very well what they are doing, but still, they are doing it" (1989b: 29).

7 As Žižek wryly notes, "I already am eating from the trashcan all the time. The name of this trashcan is ideology" (*TPGI*).
8 See Žižek's analysis, in *Christian Atheism*, of Iris from Varoufakis' novel *Another Now* (2024: 203–5).
9 It also means that *any* figure of the paranoiac Other could occupy this position of negative magnitude – as we are currently seeing in the persecution of trans people on the contemporary political scene.

Chapter 6

Conclusion

Psychoanalytic Film Thinking

Greta Gerwig's *Barbie* (2023) confirms Freud's assertion that "people never willingly abandon a libidinal position" (SE 14: 244). Freud was referring to mourning and melancholia and the difficulties of our attachments to a lost love object, but we can see how this observation holds in the socio-political sphere more generally. *Barbie* presents an ironic commentary on contemporary Western ideology at the intersections of gender discrimination and class exploitation. The film shows the appeal of ideological fantasy to be primarily affective rather than intellectual: although he borrows a few books from the library, for Ken patriarchy mainly seems to be about mini-fridges, horses, and feeling good, while his manospheric "Kendom" can be seen as a flight from symbolic castration through performative machismo. The Barbies – who have clearly read their Spinoza – recognise that such strength of feeling can only be defeated by another affect: here, jealousy, as they antagonise the Kens by flirting with their rivals and thus remind them of their lack.[1] Stereotypical Barbie, conversely, falls into a deep depression as she finds herself an object of suspicion and harassment (Fig. 6.1). This signals her encounter with contradiction – given voice by Gloria's monologue, "It is literally impossible to be a woman …" but experienced directly by Barbie's engagement with the world – and leads to her determination to embrace lack and become a subject.

We cannot simply be *talked out of* our libidinal investments. In this sense, the depiction of the Barbies being "deprogrammed" by Gloria's speech is a compromise: to narrative expediency on the

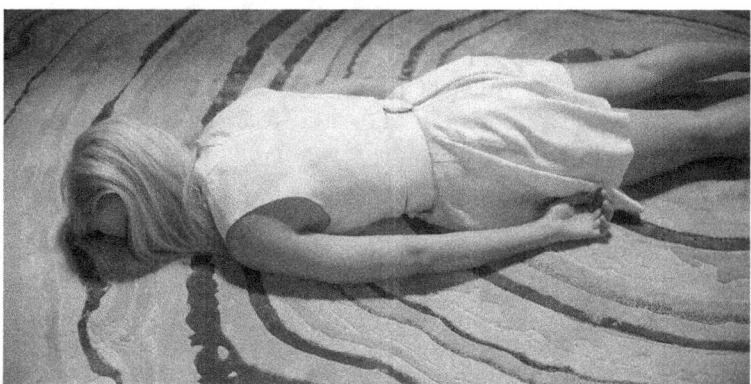

Figure 6.1 Barbie – Looking the negative in the face

one hand (*Barbie*, unlike most contemporary blockbusters, is under 2 hours long), but to a kind of neoliberal postfeminism (of capitalism and personal responsibility), on the other. Mark Fisher suggests that what is traditionally referred to as "consciousness raising" does not only replace ignorance with new knowledge but also produces a *new subject*, who becomes aware not just of the current state affairs but, crucially, of the possibility of things becoming otherwise (2018: 419–25). *Barbie* shows that this transformation requires *more* than just knowledge: it has an *affective* dimension, too. Contradiction must be subjectively assumed and worked through – one must leave Barbieland and return, not just move straight into the Weirdhouse – to bring about change.[2]

We find a similarly circuitous path in the emergence of psychoanalytic film thinking. In "The Orthopsychic Subject", Copjec references philosopher of science Gaston Bachelard's notion of the "epistemological break" – or the *discontinuity* between a previous model of knowledge and a newer one that emerges like a "rupture" – suggesting that attention to the *apparatus* of cinema (an idea, *dispositif*, itself taken from Bachelard) effected a break with film theory (1994: 19–20). Copjec also notes "two stages" in the development of semiotics (a shift marked by attention to the subject as well as the signifier) and in Freud's conception of transference, with emphasis on the analyst/analysand relationship marking the point at which "psychoanalysis (properly speaking) was begun" (239, n9). I would suggest that Copjec's own intervention – along with that of Rose, Žižek, and McGowan – constitutes a further rupture, a break with psychoanalytic film theory itself at which point *psychoanalytic film thinking (properly speaking) was begun*. Although Copjec is not a Hegelian (her commitment to Kant being a salient difference between herself and Žižek), what she articulates in her essay is the difference between *dualism* and *dialectics* that animates Žižek's project, marking it as distinct from the vision of so-called Post-Theory: change comes not from the conflict between "competing theories" in a "marketplace of ideas" but from the emergence of contradiction within the idea itself.

In this, we can recognise the dialectical necessity of first taking the *wrong* path (e.g., *screen as mirror*) and pursuing it until we reach a dead-end as its internal contradictions become apparent, from which another path emerges (*mirror as screen*) along which we mobilise contradiction itself (the gaze as point of failure within the visual field) to develop a contemporary psychoanalytic film thinking.[3] Crucially, the dialectical emergence of this new framework should *not* be understood as *evolutionary progression* from one logic to the next in what Žižek calls a "continuous course of transformations", whereby contradictions are successively overcome. Instead, dialectical movement "consists in the incessant repetition of a beginning *ex nihilo*, in the annihilation and retroactive restructuring of supposed contents" (1989b: 144–5). The successive interventions presented in this book should not therefore be considered a progressive adjustment, with, for example, Rose's initial gesture becoming iteratively honed into a singular film theory by Copjec, then Žižek, then Edelman, and so on. In one sense, it is less important to establish who published what *first* than it is to address the conceptual specificity of each approach. The mapping out of this intellectual history has been a means to that end in this book, but as Copjec herself notes, "Biography rather than theory is the source of the demand for the continuity of […] concepts" (1994: 239, n9). Each theorist makes their own attempt at harnessing concepts such as *enjoyment* and *objet a* to understand cinema, repeating, restructuring, renewing what has gone before.

Conclusion 125

The final claim of this book, then, will be for the further possibilities in developing psychoanalytic film thinking – particularly as it meets wider philosophical discourses – that may yet reshape the field. We saw Steven Shaviro claim psychoanalysis as an ally in the broader defence of Theory, and I would also look to film-philosophers such as Jenny Chamarette (2012) and Saige Walton (2016), who do not reject psychoanalysis out of hand but recognise what is useful in it to find ways of extending and multiplying accounts of cinema and phenomenology, for example. Freud, of course, observed that seeing is "an activity that is ultimately derived from touching" (SE 7: 156); and we need only note that Lacan and Merleau-Ponty were friends and interlocutors – the latter having a discernible impact on the influential Seminar XI – to appreciate that there is great potential for deeper conversations between such approaches in the realm of cinema. For example, as Colette Soler (2015) delineates, there is an established Lacanian theory of affect that could be brought into the analysis of the forms and experiences of film (particularly on anxiety); and there remains significant scope, as Kate Ince (2011) puts it, to *bring bodies back in* to the psychoanalysis of cinema, particularly in terms of notions of symptom and sexuation.

Taking on this book's insights into questions of object, enjoyment, and ideology in particular, we should now be able to open spaces for further engagement between psychoanalytic film theory and other vital contemporary discourses such as critical race theory, trans studies, and ecocriticism. What productive encounters might be staged between Ranjana Khanna's (2003) postcolonial critique of psychoanalysis, exile, and melancholia, the hauntings of Mati Diop's *Atlantics*, and the discourses of necropolitics and Afro-pessimism? How might the work of Patricia Gherovici (2017) on gender-variance and Sheila Cavanagh (2019) on the myth of Tiresias articulate with Eliza Steinbock's (2019) study of trans cinema and the aesthetics of change? What might the Lacanian understanding of jouissance in Wong Kar Wai or Céline Sciamma reveal about the libidinal underpinnings of the capitalist compulsion to *more, more, more* that brings upon us climate devastation, and how might such cine-psychoanalytic insight help us to avert this fate? This would be the stuff of a psychoanalytic film thinking to come.

Notes

1 Baruch Spinoza wrote in his *Ethics* that "An emotion cannot be restrained or taken away except through an emotion that is contrary to and stronger than the emotion that is to be restrained" ([1677] 2018: 165).
2 Similarly, Freud observed that simple *knowledge* of the unconscious has "as much influence on the symptoms of nervous illness as a distribution of menu-cards in a time of famine has upon hunger" (SE 11: 25). If the present book imparts knowledge of psychoanalysis and cinema, then this is only half the equation: psychoanalytic film thinking is a practice activated in our encounters with the screen.
3 Mulvey has also written many excellent works of psychoanalytic film theory *after* "Visual Pleasure and Narrative Cinema", such as *Fetishism and Curiosity* (1996) and *Death 24x a Second* (2006).

Recommended Reading

Lebeau, Vicky (2001) *Psychoanalysis and Cinema*. Wallflower Press. How psychoanalysis and cinema emerge at the end of the Nineteenth Century.

McGowan, Todd (2007a) *The Real Gaze*. SUNY Press. McGowan's systematic elaboration of a new psychoanalytic film thinking.

Metz, Christian (1982) *The Imaginary Signifier*. Indiana University Press. This classic text of 1970s psychoanalytic film theory remains a rich resource.

Mulvey, Laura (2006) *Death 24x a Second*. Reaktion Books. Mulvey takes psychoanalytic film theory in a new direction through photography and the death drive.

Slattery, James Lawrence (2025) *Taking Back Desire*. Routledge. New psychoanalytic film thinking through radical queer and anti-capitalist critique.

Žižek, Slavoj (2001) *The Fright of Real Tears*. BFI. Žižek's most sustained engagement with film theory and criticism. See also his *The Pervert's Guide to Cinema* (2006) and *The Pervert's Guide to Ideology* (2013) with Sophie Fiennes.

Bibliography

Adams, Parveen (1996) *The Emptiness of the Image*. Routledge.
Althusser, Louis (1971) *Lenin and Philosophy and Other Essays*. Monthly Review Press.
Ambrósio Garcia, Carla (2016) *Bion in Film Theory and Analysis*. Routledge.
Andreas-Salomé, Lou ([1913] 1964) *The Freud Journal of Lou Andreas Salomé*. Basic Books.
Bainbridge, Caroline (2019) Television as Psychical Object: Mad Men and the value of Psychoanalysis for Television Scholarship. *CST*, 14 (3), 289–306.
Balsom, Erika (2020) In Search of the Female Gaze. *Cinema Scope*. Available from: https://cinema-scope.com/features/in-search-of-the-female-gaze/ (Accessed 13 November 2024).
Baudry, Jean-Louis ([1970] 1974–1975) Ideological Effects of the Basic Cinematographic Apparatus. *Film Quarterly*, 28 (2), 39–47.
Baudry, Jean-Louis ([1975] 1976) The Apparatus. *Camera Obscura*, 1 (1), 104–126.
Beauvoir, Simone de ([1949] 2011) *The Second Sex*. Vintage.
Bellour, Raymond (2000) *The Analysis of Film*. Indiana University Press.
Berger, John (1972) *Ways of Seeing*. Penguin.
Bhabha, Homi (1984) Of Mimicry and Man: The Ambivalence of Colonial Discourse. *October*, 28, 125–133.
Bianchi, Pietro (2017) *Jacques Lacan and Cinema*. Karnac.
Bonitzer, Pascal (1982) *Le Champ aveugle*. Gallimard.
Bordwell, David & Carroll, Noël (eds.) (1996) *Post-Theory*. University of Wisconsin Press.
Bradbury-Rance, C. (2022) Lesbian Legibility and Queer Legacy in Céline Sciamma's *Portrait de la jeune fille en feu* (2019). *French Screen Studies*, 23 (2–3), 172–184.

Brey, Iris (2020) *Le Regard féminin*. Éditions de l'Olivier.
Butler, Judith (1990) *Gender Trouble*. Routledge.
Cahiers du Cinéma ([1970] 1972) John Ford's Young Mr Lincoln. *Screen*, 13 (3), 5–44.
Cavanagh, Sheila (2019) Tiresias: Bracha L. Ettinger and the Transgression with-in-to the Feminine. In Agnieszka Piotrowska and Ben Tyrer (eds.) *Femininity and Psychoanalysis*. Routledge.
Chamarette, Jenny (2012) *Phenomenology and the Future of Film*. Palgrave Macmillan.
Chion, Michel ([1982] 1999) *The Voice in Cinema*. Columbia University Press.
Cooper, Sarah (2008) Identification Today. *Nottingham French Studies*, 47 (3), 103–110.
Copjec, Joan (1994) *Read My Desire*. MIT Press.
Cowie, Elizabeth (1997) *Representing the Woman*. University of Minnesota Press.
Creed, Barbara (1993) *The Monstrous-Feminine*. Routledge.
Dayan, Daniel (1974) The Tutor-Code of Classical Cinema. *Film Quarterly*, 28 (1), 22–31.
Dean, Tim (2003) Lacan and Queer Theory. In Jean-Michel Rabaté (ed.) *The Cambridge Companion to Lacan*. Cambridge University Press.
Diawara, Manthia (1988) Black Spectatorship: Problems of Identification and Resistance. *Screen*, 29 (4), 66–79.
Doane, Mary Ann (1982) Film and the Masquerade: Theorising Female Spectatorship. *Screen*, 23 (3–4), 74–88.
Doane, Mary Ann, Mellencamp, Patricia & Williams, Linda (eds.) (1984) *Re-vision*. University Publications of America.
Dolar, Mladen (1993) Beyond Interpellation. *Qui Parle*, 6 (2), 75–96.
Dolar, Mladen (2006) *A Voice and Nothing More*. MIT Press.
Du Bois, W.E.B. ([1903] 2015) *The Souls of Black Folks*. Yale University Press.
Dyer, Richard (1997) *White*. Routledge.
Edelman, Lee (2004) *No Future*. Duke University Press.
Fanon, Frantz ([1952] 2008) *Black Skin, White Masks*. Pluto Press.
Fanon, Frantz ([1959] 2007) *A Dying Colonialism*. Trans. Grove Press.
Fanon, Frantz ([1961] 2011) *The Wretched of the Earth*. Grove Press.
Fisher, Mark (2009) *Capitalist Realism*. Zero Books.
Fisher, Mark (2018) *K-Punk*. Repeater.
Flisfeder, Matthew (2012) *The Symbolic, the Sublime, and Slavoj Žižek's Theory of Film*. Palgrave Macmillan.
Frampton, Daniel (2006) *Filmosophy*. Wallflower Press.

Freud, Sigmund (1953–1974) *The Standard Edition of the Complete Psychological Works of Sigmund Freud*, 24 vols. Hogarth Press and Institute of Psycho-Analysis.
Freud, Sigmund (1975) *Letters of Sigmund Freud*. Basic Books.
Friedlander, Jennifer (2008) *Feminine Look*. SUNY Press.
Fuery, Kelli (2018) *Wilfred Bion, Thinking, and Emotional Experience with Moving Images*. Routledge.
Fuery, Kelli (2022) *Ambiguous Cinema*. Edinburgh University Press.
Fuery, Patrick (2003) *Madness and Cinema*. Bloomsbury.
Fuss, Diana (1995) *Identification Papers*. Routledge.
George, Sheldon (2016) *Trauma and Race*. Baylor University Press.
Gherovici, Patricia (2017) *Transgender Psychoanalysis*. Routledge.
Gill, Rosalind (2006) *Gender and the Media*. Polity Press.
Gorky, Maxim ([1896] 1972) The Kingdom of Shadows. In Harry M. Geduld (ed.) *Authors on Film*. Indiana University Press.
Grose, Anouchka (2018) *From Anxiety to Zoolander*. Routledge.
Heath, Stephen (1977) Notes on Suture. *Screen*, 18 (4), 48–76.
hooks, bell (1992) *Black Looks*. South End Press.
Ince, Kate (2011) Bringing Bodies Back In: For a Phenomenological and Psychoanalytic Film Criticism of Embodied Cultural Identity. *Film-Philosophy*, 15 (1), 1–12.
Khanna, Ranjana (2003) *Dark Continents*. Duke University Press.
Kotsko, Adam (2012) *Why We Love Sociopaths*. Zero Books.
Kuhn, Annette (2013) *Little Madnesses*. I.B. Tauris.
Lacan, Jacques ([1966] 2006) *Écrits*. Norton.
Lacan, Jacques ([1973] 1977) *The Four Fundamental Concepts of Psycho-Analysis*. Norton.
Lacan, Jacques ([1975] 1998) *Encore*. Norton.
Lacan, Jacques ([1981] 1993) *The Psychoses*. Norton.
Lacan, Jacques ([2004] 2014) *Anxiety*. Polity Press.
Lebeau, Vicky (2001) *Psychoanalysis and Cinema*. Wallflower Press.
Lebeau, Vicky (2014) Mirror Images: D.W. Winnicott in the Visual Field. In Agniezska Piotrowska (ed.) *Embodied Encounters*. Routledge.
Marks, Laura U. (2000) *The Skin of the Film*. Duke University Press.
Marx, Karl & Engels, Friedrich ([1932] 1976) *The German Ideology*. Progress Publishers.
McGowan, Todd (2007a) *The Real Gaze*. SUNY Press.
McGowan, Todd (2007b) Introduction: Enjoying the Cinema. *International Journal of Žižek Studies*, 1 (3), 1–13.
McGowan, Todd (2007c) *The Impossible David Lynch*. Columbia University Press.

McGowan, Todd (2007d) There Is Nothing Lost in Translation. *Quarterly Review of Film and Video*, 24 (1), 53–64.

McGowan, Todd (2014) The Priority of the Example: Speculative Identity in Film Studies. In Louis-Paul Willis & Matthew Flisfeder (eds.) *Žižek and Media Studies*. Palgrave.

McGowan, Todd (2015) *Psychoanalytic Film Theory and The Rules of the Game*. Bloomsbury.

McGowan, Todd (2016) *Capitalism and Desire*. Columbia University Press.

McGowan, Todd (2019) *Emancipation After Hegel*. Columbia University Press.

McGowan, Todd (2020a) Interview: Politics of Moviegoing. *Crisis and Critique*, 7 (2), 298–312.

McGowan, Todd (2020b) The Gaze in Cinema. Available at https://www.youtube.com/watch?v=-ukJTaTgyQ4 (Accessed 5 December 2024).

McGowan, Todd (2020c) The Object of Silent Cinema. *Crisis and Critique* 7 (2), 228–243.

McGowan, Todd (2020d) Theories of Ideology. Available at https://www.youtube.com/watch?v=ywb_DUex9hs (Accessed 6 December 2024).

McGowan, Todd (2021) Read My Desire, Pt. 1: Gaze and Excess. *Why Theory*. Available at https://podcasts.apple.com/jo/podcast/read-my-desire-pt-1-gaze-and-excess/id1299863834?i=1000525364829 (Accessed 5 December 2024).

McGowan, Todd (2022) *The Racist Fantasy*. Bloomsbury.

McGowan, Todd (2023) History and Theory of the objet a. Available at https://www.youtube.com/watch?v=vTmVUiR7wfk (Accessed 5 December 2024).

McGowan, Todd & Kunkle, Sheila (eds.) (2004) *Lacan and Contemporary Film*. The Other Press.

Metz, Christian (1982) *The Imaginary Signifier*. Indiana University Press.

Miller, Jacques-Alain ([1966] 1977) Suture (Elements of the Logic of the Signifier). *Screen*, 18 (4), 23–34.

Mitchell, Juliet (1974) *Psychoanalysis and Feminism*. Allen Lane.

Mittell, Jason (2022) Sympathizing with Storytelling in BREAKING BAD. Available at https://vimeo.com/711303928 (Accessed 1 November 2024).

Mullarkey, John (2009) *Refractions of Reality*. Palgrave Macmillan.

Mulvey, Laura (1975) Visual Pleasure and Narrative Cinema. *Screen*, 16 (3), 6–18.

Mulvey, Laura (1981) Afterthoughts on "Visual Pleasure and Narrative Cinema" Inspired by King Vidor's Duel in the Sun (1946). *Framework*, 15–17, 12–15.

Mulvey, Laura (1996) *Fetishism and Curiosity*. BFI.

Mulvey, Laura (2006) *Death 24x a Second*. Reaktion Books.
Neale, Steve (1983) Masculinity as Spectacle. *Screen*, 24 (6), 2–17.
Neroni, Hilary (2005) *The Violent Woman*. SUNY Press.
Oudart, Jean-Pierre ([1969] 1977) Cinema and Suture. *Screen*, 18 (4), 35–47.
Penley, Constance (1989) *The Future of an Illusion*. University of Minnesota Press.
Pisters, Patricia (2012) *The Neuro-Image*. Stanford University Press.
Potter, Susan (2022) Sex Scene and Unseen: Portrait de la jeune fille en feu (Céline Sciamma, 2019). *French Screen Studies*, 23 (2–3), 185–197.
Restuccia, Frances (2012) *The Blue Box*. Continuum.
Riviere, Joan (1929) Womanliness as Masquerade. *International Journal of Psycho-Analysis*, 9, 303–313.
Rodowick, D.N. (1988) *The Crisis of Political Modernism*. University of Illinois Press.
Rose, Jacqueline (1986) *Sexuality in the Field of Vision*. Verso.
Rushton, Richard (2002) Cinema's Double: Some Reflections on Metz. *Screen*, 43 (2), 107–118.
Sabbadini, Andrea (2014) *Moving Images*. Routledge.
Sergeant, Alexander (2021) *Encountering the Impossible*. SUNY Press.
Shaheen, Jack ([2001] 2009) *Reel Bad Arabs*. Interlink.
Shaviro, Steven (1993) *The Cinematic Body*. University of Minnesota Press.
Shaviro, Steven (2008) The Cinematic Body REDUX. *Parallax*, 14 (1), 48–54.
Shohat, Ella & Stam, Robert ([1994] 2014) *Unthinking Eurocentrism*. Routledge.
Silverman, Kaja (1983) *The Subject of Semiotics*. Oxford University Press.
Silverman, Kaja (1988) *The Acoustic Mirror*. Indiana University Press.
Silverman, Kaja (1992) *Male Subjectivity at the Margins*. Routledge.
Slattery, James Lawrence (2025) *Taking Back Desire*. Routledge.
Smith, Murray (1995) *Engaging Characters*. Clarendon Press.
Smith, Murray (2011) Just What Is It That Makes Tony Soprano Such An Appealing, Attractive Murderer?. In Ward E. Jones & Samantha Vice (eds.) *Ethics at the Cinema*. Oxford University Press.
Sobchack, Vivian (1992) *The Address of the Eye*. Princeton University Press.
Sobchack, Vivian (2004) *Carnal Thoughts*. University of California Press.
Soler, Colette (2015) *Lacanian Affects*. Routledge.
Spinoza, Baruch ([1677] 2018) *Ethics*. Cambridge University Press.
Steinbock, Eliza (2019) *Shimmering Images*. Duke University Press.
Stone, Rob (2014) *Spanish Cinema*. Routledge.

Studlar, Gaylyn (1993) *In the Realm of Pleasure*. Columbia University Press.

Tyrer, Ben (2014) An Atheist's Guide to Feminine Jouissance: On *Black Swan* and the Other Satisfaction. In Agniezska Piotrowska (ed.) *Embodied Encounters*. Routledge.

Tyrer, Ben (2016) *Out of the Past*. Palgrave Macmillan.

Tyrer, Ben (2017) This Tongue is Not my Own: Dogtooth, Phobia and the Paternal Metaphor. In Tonia Kazakopoulou & Mikela Fotiou (eds.) *Contemporary Greek Film Cultures from 1990 to the Present*. Peter Lang.

Tyrer, Ben (2019) Under Her Skin: On Woman without Body and Body without Woman. In Agniezska Piotrowska & Ben Tyrer (ed.) *Femininity and Psychoanalysis*. Routledge.

Tyrer, Ben (2022) The Shudder-Image: Psych-Soma, Sex and Knowledge in Hannibal. *Screen*, 63 (4), 464–494.

Tyrer, Ben (2023) That Obscure Object of Ontology: Lacan, La femme, Lathouse and Her. In Martin Bartelmus & Friederike Danebrock (eds.) *Therapie der Dinge?*. Transcript.

Vaage, Margrethe Bruun (2015) *The Antihero in American Television*. Routledge.

Vighi, Fabio (2009) *Sexual Difference in European Cinema*. Palgrave Macmillan.

Walton, Saige (2016) *Cinema's Baroque Flesh*. Amsterdam University Press.

Willis, Sharon (1993) Hardware and Hardbodies, What Do Women Want? A Reading of Thelma and Louise. In Jim Collins et al. (eds.) *Film Theory Goes to the Movies*. Routledge.

Wollen, Peter (1982) *Readings and Writings*. Verso.

Wynter, Kevin (2022) *Critical Race Theory and Jordan Peele's Get Out*. Bloomsbury.

Yates, Candida (2007) *Masculine Jealousy and Contemporary Cinema*. Palgrave MacMillan.

Žižek, Slavoj (1986) Hitchcock. *October*, 38, 99–111.

Žižek, Slavoj (1989a) The Undergrowth of Enjoyment: How Popular Culture Can Serve as an Introduction to Lacan. *New Formations*, 9, 7–29.

Žižek, Slavoj (1989b) *The Sublime Object of Ideology*. Verso.

Žižek, Slavoj (1991a) *Looking Awry*. MIT Press.

Žižek, Slavoj (1991b) *For They Know Not What They Do*. Verso.

Žižek, Slavoj (1992a) In His Bold Gaze My Ruin Is Writ Large. In Slavoj Žižek (ed.) *Everything You Always Wanted to Know About Lacan (But Were Afraid to Ask Hitchcock)*. Verso.

Žižek, Slavoj (1992b) *Enjoy Your Symptom!*. Routledge.

Žižek, Slavoj (1993) *Tarrying with the Negative*. Duke University Press.

Žižek, Slavoj (1994) A Hair of the Dog That Bit You. In Mark Bracher et al. (eds.) *Lacanian Theory of Discourse*. New York University Press.
Žižek, Slavoj ([1997a] 2008) *The Plague of Fantasies*, 2nd edn. Verso.
Žižek, Slavoj (1997b) *The Plague of Fantasies*. Verso.
Žižek, Slavoj (1999) The Thing from Inner Space. Available at https://www.lacan.com/zizekthing.htm (Accessed 28 October 2024).
Žižek, Slavoj (2000) *The Art of the Ridiculous Sublime*. University of Washington Press.
Žižek, Slavoj (2001) *The Fright of Real Tears*. BFI.
Žižek, Slavoj (2002) The Real of Sexual Difference. In Suzanne Barnard & Bruce Fink (eds.) *Reading Seminar XX*. SUNY Press.
Žižek, Slavoj (2006) *How to Read Lacan*. Granta.
Žižek, Slavoj (2012a) *Less than Nothing*. Verso.
Žižek, Slavoj (2012b) "Suture", Forty Years Later. In Peter Hallward & Knox Peden (eds.) *Concept and Form*, vol. 2. Verso.
Žižek, Slavoj (2016a) *Disparities*. Bloomsbury.
Žižek, Slavoj (2016b) In Conversation with Slavoj Žižek TIFF 2016. Available at https://www.youtube.com/watch?v=lh07tJMR-3c (Accessed 4 December 2024).
Žižek, Slavoj (2017) *Incontinence of the Void*. MIT Press.
Žižek, Slavoj (2019) *Sex and the Failed Absolute*. Bloomsbury.
Žižek, Slavoj (2024) *Christian Atheism*. Bloomsbury.
Zupančič, Alenka (2008) *Why Psychoanalysis?*. NSU Press.
Zupančič, Alenka (2017) *What Is Sex?*. MIT Press.

Index

Note: Page numbers in *italics* indicate figures, and references following "n" refer to the notes.

120 BPM (2017) 93
45 years (2015) 33

accumulation 114, 117
acousmatic voice 90, 108
The Acoustic Mirror (Silverman) 89–90
The Address of the Eye (Sobchack) 6
aesthetics, theory of 63
Afro-pessimism 125
Akerman, Chantal 42
Algerian revolution 30–32
"Algeria Unveiled" (Fanon) 31–32
alienation effect 100
All that Heaven Allows (1955) 56–57
al-Mansour, Haifaa 33
Althusser, Louis 100, 101, 103–104, 120n3
Amazon 61
The Ambassadors painting (1533) 64, 67, 75
Ambiguous Cinema (Fuery) 54
Amélie (2001) 62
American Psycho (2000) 37
American Sniper (2014) 31, 33, 106
Andreas-Salomé, Lou 7n2
Andress, Ursula 57
anti-Semitism 62, 117–120

anxiety 36, 71, 78; castration 48, 88, 125
Apparatus theory 28, 54, 69, 78, 101
Arnold, Andrea 5, 21, 93–94
Arzner, Dorothy 49
Ashby, Hal 59
Atlantics (2019) 33, *33*, 125
aural perception 91

bacall, Lauren 43
Bachelard, Gaston 123
Balsom, Erika 51, 53
Barbie (2023) 122–123, *123*
The Battle of Algiers (1966) 32
Baudry, Jean-Louis 5, 9–14, 16, 22, 23, 28, 43, 44, 100, 106; "Ideological Effects of the Basic Cinematographic Apparatus" 9, 20, 100; about mirror image 19–21
Bay, Michael 47
Bazin, André 24
A Beautiful Mind (2001) 87
Beau Travail (1999) 53
Beauvoir, Simone de 42, 54

Bellour, Raymond 3, 54
Bentham, Jeremy 70
Berger, John 41, 47, 59
Bergman, Ingrid 76
"Beyond Interpellation" (Dolar) 103
Bhabha, Homi 30
Bianchi, Pietro 39n4
The Big Sleep (1946) 112
bird's-eye view shot 76
The Birth of a Nation (1915) 31, 87
blackness 60–61, 62
Black Panther (2018) 61
Black Skin, White Masks (Fanon) 29
The Blue Box (Restuccia) 92
Blue is the Warmest Colour (2013) 53
Blue Velvet (1986) 45, 88–89
Bonitzer, Pascal 72–73
Bordwell, David 7, 34–35, 97–99, 124
Bradbury-Rance, Clara 53
Breaking the Waves (1996) 74
Brecht, Bertolt 100
Bresson, Robert 107
Brey, Iris 6, 51–52, 69
Brown, Clarence 15
Buñuel, Luis 8
Butler, Judith 51

Cahiers du Cinéma 3, 24, 100
Campion, Jane 29
Capitalism and Desire (McGowan) 112–113
capitalism 33, 37, 39n6, 98, 104, 111, 117, 123, 125; and enjoyment 112–116
capitalist realism 111
capitonnage 2
Carpenter, John 96, 110
Carroll, Noël 7, 34–35, 97–99, 124
Casino Royale (2006) 57–58, *58*
castration 48, 56, 59, 88
Cavanagh, Sheila 125
Cemetery of Splendour (2015) 8
Chamarette, Jenny 125

Chaplin, Charlie 74
Chion, Michel 72–73, 89–90, 108
"Cinema and Suture" (Oudart) 106
cinema-spectator relationship, 19–21; *see also* identification
The Cinematic Body (Shaviro) 6, 99
cinematic thinking 74
Citizen Kane (1941) 108
City Lights (1931) 74
class struggle 108
Cocoon (1985) 87
Coeur fidèle (1923) 25
cognitive film theory 35–36
cognitivism 3
colonisation 29–34
Coming Home (1978) 59
common sense 16, 20, 38
competition 37, 56
complex television 36
Confucius 34
consciousness raising 123
constitutive incompleteness 106
contemplative cinema 25
The Conversation (1974) 91–92
Coogler, Ryan 61
Cooper, Sarah 28
Copjec, Joan 5–6, 64, 69–72, 79, 82, 83, 101–103, 123–124; "The Orthopsychic Subject: Film Theory and the Reception of Lacan" 6, 69–72, 79, 101–102, 123; "Sex and the Euthanasia of Reason" 92
Coppola, Sofia 34
corporeal identification 29
counter-cinema 101, 120n4
Cousins, Mark 8
Cowie, Elizabeth 5, 51
Craig, Daniel 57
Creed, Barbara 58, 63n3
Curtis, Adam 22
cynicism 120n6

Dali, Salvador 8
Dance, Girl, Dance (1940) 49

Dash, Julie 61
Daughters of the Dust (1991) 61
Dayan, Daniel 107
Dean, Tim 93
Decalogue 6 (1989) 109
Deleuze, Gilles 7
delusion 67
Denis, Claire 53
Deren, Maya 3, 8
desire 11, 15, 34, 52, 77–89, 91–93, 102, 113–114; objects of desire 46, 50, 66–68, 82, 118
Desnos, Robert 8
dialectics 92
Diawara, Manthia 31, 60, 61
Dickens, Charles 16
Diesel, Vin 56
difference 41, 70, 117; elision of 28; oppositional gaze 59–63; sexual 41–42, 44, 53, 92–95
differend 99
Diop, Mati 33, 125
Disparities (Žižek) 16
Doane, Mary Ann 50–51, 61
Dogtooth (2009) 38
Dolar, Mladen 90, 103–104
Do the Right Thing (1989) 86–87
Double Indemnity (1944) 48
The Double Life of Veronique (1991) 109
dream: of cinema 13–14; dream-cave 9–13, 100; as metaphor 8–9; screen of 14–17
Dream Productions (2024) 8
Dr No (1962) 57
Dr Strangelove (1964) 86
Du Bois, W.E.B. 60
Duel in the Sun (1946) 49
Dulac, Germaine 8
Dune (1984) 91
Dyer, Richard 62

Edelman, Lee 6, 54, 93, 124
Edinburgh Film Festival 42

ego 19, 120n2; bodily 103; formation 24; ideal ego 19, 44, 54–56, 65, 66; and identification 25; masculine 57; spectatorial 24
ego psychology 98
Emily in Paris (2020) 62
enjoyment (*jouissance*) 5, 37, 50, 60, 72, 82–89, 93, 111, 112–116, 124
Enter the Void (2009) 27–28
Epstein, Jean 25
Erice, Victor 11
exhibitionism 45

false consciousness 96, 104, 110–111
Fanon, Frantz 29; "Algeria Unveiled" 31–32; *The Wretched of the Earth* 30
fantasy 43, 85–88, 111–112, 119
Fassbinder, Rainer Werner 59, 69
Fast and Furious 56
Fellini, Federico 86
female gaze 51–54
Feminine Look (Friedlander) 92
femininity 49–51, 58, 92
fetishism 48, 50
Fiennes, Sophie 73, 80
Fifty Shades of Grey (2015) 25
Fight Club (1999) 25
film language 25, 52
film sound 72–77
Film Studies 3, 34–35, 97, 106; Anglophone 40, 73; apparatus theory 28, 71
Fisher, Mark 6, 111, 123
Forbidden Planet (1956) 15
Foreign Correspondent (1940) 75
Foucault, Michel 69–71
Fox, Megan 47, 51
Frammartino, Michelangelo 5, 25
Frankenstein (1931) 12
Freud, Sigmund 2–4, 9–11, 19, 25, 29, 33, 41, 43, 45, 48, 63n3, 67, 68, 75, 92, 98, 105, 122, 125;

femininity theory 49; lost object 66; psychosexual stages 75
Friedlander, Jennifer 92
The Fright of Real Tears (Žižek) 97, 107
Fuery, Kelli 54
Fuery, Patrick 39n3
Full Metal Jacket (1987) 86
Fuss, Diana 29, 30–31, 34

Gance, Abel 27
gaze 70, 76–77; female 51–54; look and 68–69; male 43–49, 53, 68, 87; oppositional 59–63; panoptic 70; politics of 103–106; and voice 72–73; white 61, 95n7
George, Sheldon 6, 86
Gerwig, Greta 122
Gherovici, Patricia 125
Gilda (1946) 51
Godard, Jean-Luc 101, 107
Gorin, Jean-Pierre 101
Gorky, Maxim 8
Griffith, D.W. 31, 87
Grose, Anouchka 3
Guy, Alice 49

Haigh, Andrew 33
hallucination 10, 11
Haynes, Todd 40
Hays Code of censorship 18, 111–112
Hayworth, Rita 51
His Girl Friday (1940) 48
Hitchcock, Alfred 3, 8, 20, 81
Hogg, Joanna 1, 5, 40
Holbein, Hans 64, 75, 80
Hollywood 5, 17, 31, 41–44, 46, 63, 87, 90
homoeroticism 56–57
hooks, bell 6, 60
Howard, Ron 87
Hudson, Rock 56–57

identification 18, 32, 54, 79, 101; colonisation vs 29–34; politics of 32; primary 20, 23–27, 34, 44; radical over 38; reflections 28–29; screen mirror 19–21, 65; secondary 20, 24, 25–26, 32, 34, 36; strange mirror 21–28; sympathy for devil/villain 34–39; tertiary/intra-diegetic level of 55
"Ideological Effects of the Basic Cinematographic Apparatus" 9, 20, 100
ideology 42, 73, 95, 96, 122, 125; anti-Semitism and 117–120; capitalism and enjoyment 112–116; cinematic apparatus 100–101; gaze politics 103–106; against imaginary relation 101–103; Lacanian view 97–99; limitations in 109–112; suture 106–109
Illusions (1982) 61
The Imaginary Signifier (Metz) 21–24, 40, 97
immorality 36–37
The Impossible David Lynch (McGowan) 88
Ince, Kate 125
Inception (2010) 8
integration, cinema of 87–88, 104
interface 108–109
interpellation 100, 103, 108, 120n3
intersection, cinema of 88–89, 104
intervention, in conversations 1–2
In The Mood for Love (2000) 84–85, *85*
Iron Man (2008) 31
irrationality 38

Jacques Lacan and Cinema (Bianchi) 39n4
James Bond 57–58
Jaws (1975) 55, 87, 117

Jeanne Dielman, 23 quai du Commerce, 1080 Bruxelles (1975) 42–43
Jenkins, Barry 61
Jennifer's Body (2009) 51
Johnson, Dwayne 56

Keaton, Buster 14
Kechiche, Abdellatif 53
Khanna, Ranjana 125
Kieslowski, Krzysztof 16, 108–109
The Killers (1946) 98
KKK violence 31, 87
Kotsko, Adam 37
Kubrick, Stanley 86
Kunkle, Sheila 97

Lacan, Jacques 1–7, 24, 25, 41–43, 80, 82, 88, 97–99, 102–103, 119; *Anxiety* 88; *The Four Fundamental Concepts of Psycho-Analysis*, 64–73, 71, 79, 101, 107, 125; *Encore* 92; mirror stage 19–21, 67; "Remarks on Daniel Lagache" 65; theorisation of "*objet a*" 64, 66, 79
La chute de la maison Usher (1928) 25
Lady in the Lake (1947) 27, 28
Lang, Fritz 89–90
Lanthimos, Yorgos 38
Las Meninas painting (1656) 109
Lebeau, Vicky 39n2, 73
Lee, Spike 60, 61–62, 86
Le Quattro Volte (2010) 25–26
Le regard féminin (Brey) 51–52
Levinas, Emmanuel 34
Lewin, Bertram 9
Looking Awry (Žižek) 95n3
Lost Highway (1997) 8, 78
Lost in Translation (2003) 34, 91
Lupino, Ida 49
Lynch, David 3, 8, 45, 73; Lynchian nightmare 46
Lyotard, Jean-Francois 99

M (1931) 89–90
Magic Mike XXL (2015) 53
The Magnificent Ambersons (1942) 90
male gaze 43–49, 53, 68, 87
Male Subjectivity at the Margins (Silverman) 58–59
Manhattan (1979) 62
Mann, Anthony 57
Mann, Michael 86
manosphere 18
The Man Who Shot Liberty Valance (1962) 55
marginal masculinities 58–59
Marks, Laura U. 94
Marnie (1964) 8
Marxism 100, 108
masculinisation 49–50
masculinity 92; narcissistic 54–55; and visual pleasure 54–58
masochism 50, 57
mastery 54, 69, 98; bodily 19; failure of 83–84, 105; visual 102–103
The Matrix (1999) 110–111
McGowan, Todd 5, 17n1, 34, 64, 73, 77, 78–80, 92, 94, 97, 115, 116, 117, 119; *Capitalism and Desire* 112–113; cinema of desire 84–85, 91; cinema of fantasy 85–86, 88; cinema of integration 87–88, 104; cinema intersection 88–89, 104; about ideology 104–105; *The Impossible David Lynch* (2007) 88; object 64; politics of gaze 104–106; *The Real Gaze* 82–89, 91; theorisation of gaze 80–84; voice as object 91–92
melodrama 51, 54
Merleau-Ponty, Maurice 7, 28, 125
Meshes of the Afternoon (1943) 8
metempsychosis 25
Metz, Christian 5, 79; *The Imaginary Signifier* 21–24, 40,

97; primary cinematic identification 25–27, 44; theory of cinematic perception 67
Miller, Jacques-Alain 106, 107–108
mirror 39n2; image 19–21, 43, 54, 65–66, 102–103; as screen 65, 69–72, 100, 124; strange 21–28, 79
misinterpretations 43
misrecognition 19, 24
Mitchell, Juliet 41
Mittell, Jason 37
Momoa, Jason 56
monstrous-feminine 63n3
Montgomery, Robert 27
moral evaluation 36
Morley, Carol 3
Mulholland Drive (2000) 91
Mullarkey, John 73, 99
Mulvey, Laura 5, 40–42, 50, 52, 55–56, 58, 59–63, 90, 92, 97; *Afterthoughts* on Visual Pleasure 49–51, 54; feminist filmmaking practice 51; male gaze theory 43–49, 53, 68, 87; "Visual Pleasure and Narrative Cinema" 49, 54, 87–88

Napoleon (1927) 27
narcissism 43–44, 101
narcissistic masculinity 54
Neale, Steve 54–56
Neeson, Liam 55
neoliberal capitalism 111, 117
Neroni, Hilary 92
Nickel Boys (2024) 27
Noé, Gaspar 27, 83
No Future (Edelman) 93
Nolan, Christopher 3, 8
normative ethics 36, 37
North By Northwest (1959) 54, 93
Notorious (1946) 76
Notting Hill (1999) 62

object 16, 22, 27, 43–49, 56, 64; look and gaze 68–69; mirror as screen 69–72; object-voice 89–92; psychoanalytic film theory 65–68; *The Real Gaze* 82–89, 91; real of sexual difference 92–95; tracking shots 77–82; Žižekian blot 72–77
Oedipal trajectory 54–55
oppositional gaze 59–63
"The Orthopsychic Subject" (Copjec) 69, 102, 123
otherness 34, 68
Oudart, Jean-Pierre 106–107
over-identification 38, 50

Paddington (2014) 14
panoptic gaze 70
Paranoia and Moral Panics (2010) 22
Parks and Recreation (2009–2015) 40
patriarchal ideology 42
The Pervert's Guide documentaries 80; *The Pervert's Guide to Cinema* (2006) 9, 15, 73, 120; *The Pervert's Guide to Ideology* (2013) 73, 96, 110
phenomenology 24
photogénie 25
The Piano (1993) 29
Pixar 8
The Plague of Fantasies (Žižek) 118
Plato 9–10
point-of-view shot 27, 107
Polley, Sarah 3
Pontecorvo, Gillo 32
Portrait of a Lady on Fire (2019) 52–53, *53*, 93
Possessed (1931) 15, 16
Post-Theory (Bordwell & Carroll) 7, 34–35, 97–99, 124
Potter, Susan 53
primary cinematic identification 23–27, 34, 44
Psycho (1960) 74, 78, 81, 90
Puenzo, Lucía 53

queerness 53, 58, 92–93

racist ideology 86
radical over-identification 38
Ramsay, Lynne 14
Ratcatcher (1999) 14
Ray, Man 8
Rear Window (1954) 20, 81
recognition 35 *see also* misrecognition
Red Road (2006) 21, 93–94, *94*
regression 10–11
reproductive futurism 54, 93
Restuccia, Frances 92
reverse tracking shot 76, 107
Riddles of the Sphinx (1977) 42
Riley, Boots 5, 112
Riviere, Joan 50–51
Rose, Jacqueline 5, 64, 65, 106, 124
Ross, RaMell 27
Rushton, Richard 97

Sabbadini, Andrea 3
sadism 48
Sciamma, Céline 5, 52–53, 125
scopophilia 43, 48
Screen journal 6, 40, 97, 106
screen mirror 19–21, 65, 69–72, 100, 124
Screen theory 65, 69, 78, 80, 89, 94, 102, 104–105, 108
secondary cinematic identification 20, 24, 25–26, 32, 34, 36
self-sabotaging subjects 83
sexual difference 41, 44, 53, 59–60, 84, 92–95
Sexual Difference in European Cinema (Vighi) 92
Sexuality in the Field of Vision (Rose) 64
Seyrig, Delphine 42
Shadow of a Doubt (1943) 76
Shaheen, Jack 31
Sharp Objects (2018) 93
Shaviro, Steven 6, 28, 99, 125
Sherlock Jr. (1924) 14

The Silence of the Lambs (1991) 89, 109
Silverman, Kaja 68–69, 107; *The Acoustic Mirror* 89–90; *Male Subjectivity at the Margins* 58–59
Singin' in the Rain (1952) 90
Sirk, Douglas 56
Slattery, James Lawrence 93
Sloterdijk, Peter 120n6
slow cinema 25
Smith, Murray 35
Sobchack, Vivian 6, 28
social masculinity 55
sociopath 37–38
Solaris (1972) 15
Soler, Colette 125
The Sopranos (1999–2007) 36
Sorry to Bother You (2018) 55, 112, 114–116, *113*
The Souvenir Part II (2021) 1–2, *2*
spectatorship 10, 20, 23, 28–29, 35, 36, 45, 62–63, 101
Spellbound (1945) 8
Spielberg, Steven 8, 83, 87, 91
Spinoza, Baruch 122, 126n1
The Spirit of the Beehive (1973) 11–12, *12*
Stalker (1979) 15
Star Wars (1977) 15
Steinbock, Eliza 125
Stewart, James 55
Stone, Rob 12
The Story of Film: A New Generation (2021) 8
strange mirror 21–28
The Sublime Object of Ideology (Žižek) 73, 117
subject, psychoanalytic 10, 19, 28, 34, 59, 66, 68, 71, 77, 80, 84, 85, 86, 90, 99, 101–103, 106, 122–123
suture 17, 106–109
"Suture (Elements of the Logic of the Signifier)" (Miller) 106

sympathy 34–39; and alignment 35, 79; and allegiance 35; for devil/villain 34–39; spectator 29; structure 35

Taking Back Desire (Slattery) 93
Tarzan 30–31, 33
The Testament of Doctor Mabuse (1933) 91
They Live (1988) 96, 110–111
"The Thing from Inner Space" (Žižek) 14
Third Cinema 13, 17n2, 32
The Thirteenth Floor (1999) 106
Three Colours: Blue (1993) 109
Titanic (1997) 16
To Have and Have Not (1944) 44
Tomboy (2011) 53
Toronto International Film Festival 74
Torrent, Ana 12–13
Tout va bien (1972) 101
tracking shot 75–76, 107
transcendental subject 20, 23, 28, 67, 100, 101–102
trans cinema 125
Transformers (2007) 47, *47*, 63
"The Tutor Code of Classical Cinema" (Dayan) 107
Twin Peaks (1990–1991) 91

unconscious 10, 11, 120n2; and cinema 13; vs common sense 38; desire 45, 67; and dreams 8; enjoyment (*jouissance*) 82, 115; fantasy 86, 119; and ideology 105; knowledge of 126n2; as "other scene" 4; patriarchal 42, 46, 48, 52; radicality of 98
The Underground Railroad (2021) 61

Vaage, Margrethe Bruun 36
Velázquez, Diego 109
Vent d'est (1970) 101, 107
Vertigo (1958) 46, 47

Vidor, King 49
Vighi, Fabio 92
violence 56, 58
The Violent Woman (Neroni) 92
visual pleasure 42, 43, 46, 48, 49, 54–58, 62
"Visual Pleasure and Narrative Cinema" (Mulvey) 49, 54, 87–88
A Voice and Nothing More (Dolar) 90
von Trier, Lars 74
voyeurism 43–45, 48, 53, 57

Wadjda (2012) 33
Walton, Saige 125
Wayne, John 55
Weerasethakul, Apichatpong 8
Whales, James 12
white feminism 60
white gaze 61, 95n7
white visual pleasure 62
Why We Love Sociopaths (2012) 37
Willemen, Paul 57
Willis, Sharon 29
Winnicott, D. W. 22–23
The Wizard of Oz (1939) 14, 87, 88, 91
Wollen, Peter 42, 120n4
"Womanliness as Masquerade" (Riviere) 50
women 31, 60, 90; under patriarchy 70; shown as visual pleasure 41, 43, 46, 48–49; under-representation of 52
Wong Kar Wai 5, 84, 91, 125
The Wretched of the Earth (Fanon) 30
Wright, Teresa 76

xxy (2007) 53

Žižek, Slavoj 5–6, 9, 14–17, 34, 38, 50, 62, 64, 72–77, *81*, 80–82, 98–99, 107–112, 117–120; blot 73–77; *Disparities* 16; *The*

Fright of Real Tears 97, 107; "Hitchcock" 73, 75; "Hitchcockian cut" 95n5, interface 108–109; *Looking Awry* 95n3; *The Pervert's Guide to Cinema* 9, 15, 73, 120; *The Pervert's Guide to Ideology* 73, 96, 110; *The Sublime Object of Ideology* 73, 117; *The Plague of Fantasies* 118; theorisation of gaze 77–82; theorisation of ideology 109–112

Zupančič, Alenka 4, 5; *What is Sex?* (2017) 92